22 Insights For Writing The
Right Book To Find New Clients Now!

MARKETING

WITH A

BOOK

FOR AGENCY OWNERS

HENRY J. DeVRIES

INDIE BOOKS
INTERNATIONAL

INDIE BOOKS INTERNATIONAL®, INC.
2511 WOODLANDS WAY
OCEANSIDE, CA 92054
www.indiebooksintl.com

CONTENTS

FOREWORD

As an agency owner, the quest to find new clients is always on your mind. My rise on Madison Avenue taught me that.

I got my start at the legendary Doyle Dane Bernbach, a $1-billion-in-billings agency that helped inspire the TV series *Mad Men*. I went on to build Buckley DeCerchio Cavalier—a creative boutique featured on the cover of the Sunday *New York Times* as one of the top ten most creative ad agencies in America.

As EVP of Strategic Planning at the advertising agency McCann Erickson Worldwide, at the time the world's largest advertising agency, I founded The 14th Floor as McCann's entrance into brand consulting. It has been my privilege to be involved with creating and launching some of the most exciting and prominent brands of our time, including Snapple, Qwest, and AT&T Business, and rebranding such leading global companies as Exxon/Esso, Motorola, and Samsung.

I left to start BrightMark Consulting to broadly apply branding to build value across global enterprises, private companies, government agencies, nonprofits, and new ventures. BrightMark's clients have included American Express, the US Navy, GE, IBM, Sotheby's, Boston Children's Hospital, US Department of State, Havas Worldwide, and iRobot.

Finding new clients has always been a key concern. Fellow agency owners can profit from the advice in this book to make business development regular, not random. I have served on the boards of the Pardee RAND Graduate School, Nemours Children's Health System, and the American Composers Orchestra, have taught as adjunct faculty at the Yale School of Management and NYU's Stern School of Management, and have been a keynote speaker at events and conferences. I have published a blog with podcasts called Overhead Space that reach over 50,000 leaders and professionals each month. Now, during these times of momentous cultural changes, spurred in part by the pandemic, global social activism, and climate change, I turned my attention to helping business leaders navigate this new world with my 2022 book, *The Enchanted Brand: The Human Side of Business in a World of New Essentialism,* which Henry and his Indie Books team published. The time was right to share my view of the world, and if you have not published a book yet I advise you to study these pages so you can share your wisdom with prospective clients.

If you have written a book, please heed Henry's advice: books don't promote authors; authors promote books. As a fellow author, let me say now is the time for us to get working on our second book. When it comes to books, thought leaders are not one and done. I wish you the best on your journey.

Jane Cavalier Lucas
Brightmark Consulting

PREFACE

Dear Small To Midsized Agency Owner:

This is the book I promised I would write you when I began my research project twenty years ago into how smart agency owners attract right-fit clients.

Today, in these uncertain times, there is something that all agencies need: more new clients. These are emotional times and to connect with clients and become influential you need to be a storyteller.

Hi, I'm Henry DeVries, and as a Forbes.com columnist who covers marketing, I see how most agency owners talk about their work in the same drab way. But there is one hidden asset that will set you apart, something nobody else is offering: *your defining stories*.

When writing my international McGraw-Hill bestseller *How to Close a Deal Like Warren Buffett*, I discovered how Buffett uses stories to persuade, gain media coverage, and become a world-famous brand.

Currently, as the CEO of Indie Books International, and author and editor of over three hundred nonfiction books, I encourage agency owners to do what Hollywood does. Over the last twenty years I have trained thousands of agency owners and consultants on how to use storytelling to attract prospects, close the sale, and cement client relationships.

After twenty years of research, the results are clear on how to attract new clients: writing the right book is the number one marketing tool; speaking about the book is the number one marketing strategy. History has taught us this, from giants such as David Ogilvy, Al Reis, Jack Trout, and more.

Discoveries in neuroscience prove decision-making is emotional, not logical. So how can you persuade the emotional part of the brain? The answer is to turn testimonials into stories that prove how you take clients from problems to solutions.

Many examples (I would never be so boring to call them case studies) are in this book for your own R&D (rob and duplicate). Write the right book and you will be amazed at how you can turn prospects into lifelong business relationships.

Henry DeVries
Oceanside, California

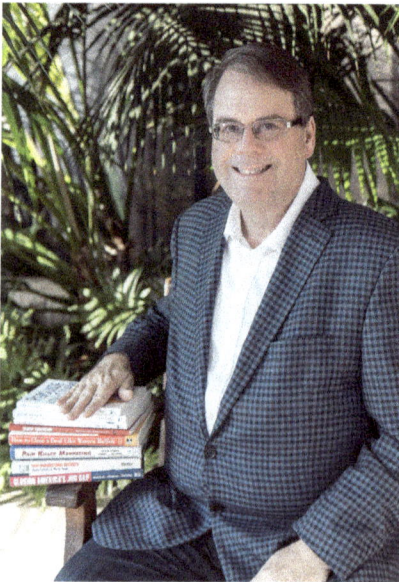

Photo by Jeff Emerson

PART I

The Why

"McDonald's says the key to happiness is you deserve a break today, but Fruit of the Loom says the key to happiness is nice undies. On the other hand, Coca-Cola says…"

1

Why Finding New Clients Is A Big Pain

Startling statistic: for three out of five agency owners, the number one pain point is finding new clients.[1] The 2018 HubSpot survey this factoid came from focused on hundreds of marketing agencies with five to two hundred employees.

Yes, agency owners wake up in the middle of the night thinking of how to find enough new clients, and not just any clients. You want right-fit clients. Let me share some hard truths about that quest:

Hard truth: The surest and fastest path to get impact and influence is to write the right book, which is no easy task. But wait, agency owners are great communicators? Ironically, many agency owners feel writing and publishing a book is too time-consuming, expensive, or undignified. Even if they tried writing, most agency owners are frustrated by a lack of results. They even worry if marketing with a book will ever work for them.

And no wonder. According to former Harvard Business School professor David Maister, the typical sales and marketing tactics that work for retailers and manufacturers are a waste of time and money for agencies because these tactics actually make them less attractive to prospective clients.[2] But agencies willing to write the right book have found it gives them more impact and influence with prospective clients. As evidence, this book is filled with examples.

Hard truth: Offer research, not rehash. You cannot just spew the same old advice to create the right book. To find new clients, the best approach for agencies is to demonstrate expertise by generously sharing valuable information through writing and speaking. The secret ingredient is to conduct research that shows prospects how they compare to their peers. For agencies this is what I believe with my heart of hearts: the number one marketing tool is a book and the number one marketing strategy is a speech. Research shows agencies can fill a pipeline with qualified prospects in as little as thirty days by offering advice and research to right-fit prospects on how to overcome their most pressing problems.[3]

AGENCIES WILLING TO WRITE THE RIGHT BOOK HAVE FOUND IT GIVES THEM MORE IMPACT AND INFLUENCE WITH PROSPECTIVE CLIENTS

Hard truth: Effort must be regular, not random. Random acts of kindness are good, and random acts of marketing are bad. What should agencies do to find new clients on a regular basis? First, understand that generating leads is an investment and should be measured like any other investment. Next, quit wasting money on ineffective means like brochures, advertising, and sponsorships. The best marketing investment agencies can make is to leverage the content in the right book. This includes sending out copies of the book, doing showcase speeches for no fee, creating informative websites, hosting persuasive seminars, booking speaking engagements, and getting published as an industry expert columnist. In a phrase, thought leadership. Thought leaders are people who write and speak about a subject and are quoted by others.

Hard truth: Your stories are a hidden asset. You might start by writing how-to blogs and articles. Those articles turn into speeches and seminars. Eventually, you gather the articles and publish a book through a strategy called print-on-demand independent publishing (we've done it in under ninety days for agencies). You have hidden assets no other agency has: your client mess-to-success stories that you helped make happen.[4] Hint: you are not the hero in these hero-quest stories; you need to accept the role of the mentor character. You are Yoda, not Luke Skywalker.

Hard truth: No investment, no return on investment. Even if you believe in the Marketing With A Book Model, how do you find time to do it and still get client and administrative work done? No agency owner ever believes they have too much time on their hands. Here is a statistic that is not startling: according to that 2018 HubSpot survey previously mentioned, the second biggest pain for almost half of the agency owners is finding time to conduct business development. This is ironically referred to as Cobbler's

Children Syndrome. Here is how therapist Ben Dattner, PhD, described it in *Psychology Today*:

> In many organizations I have encountered during my consulting career, people have complained about "Cobbler's Children Syndrome." Like the proverbial children of the shoemaker who go without shoes, I have consulted to technology companies that have outdated computer systems, marketing firms that don't market themselves in any way, and consulting firms that fail to put into practice for themselves a single theory or model upon which they have built their businesses. [5]

The cobbler's children never found that fable amusing. Neither do your agency employees find it amusing when the agency owner does not do enough to market the agency.

Nothing worth happening in business ever just happens. The answer is to carve out the time for writing a book. You need to be involved, but you should not do this all on your own. Trial and error are too expensive of a learning method. Wouldn't it be better if someone helped you who knows the tricks and shortcuts? Find someone who can show you how to leverage your time and get others to do most of the work.

Hard truth: Amazon changed the game. The good news is you do not need to get past the gatekeepers of traditional big publishing houses; you can independently publish the book. There are challenges, of course. Because print-on-demand paperback books are not typically stocked on bookstore shelves, agency authors need to do an excellent job of marketing through publicity, direct mail, and social media. But if you are willing to be a self-promoter and your book targets an identifiable market, then independent publishing may be right for you.

Hard truth: Better to write than get it right. Done is better than perfect. Any book worth writing is worth writing a first draft that sucks. We call it the sloppy first copy. The magic is in the rewrite. What about the writing? If you can author articles, then you can write a book. And if you can't, hire a freelance ghostwriter to help you do it. The only aspect you cannot outsource is the insights. You need that supercomputer that sits on the top of your neck to come up with the insights that will prove to prospects you are worth talking to about how you help companies like theirs. Agency authors tell me repeatedly that the book effort clarified their thinking on their expertise. In the words of author Joan Didion, "I don't know what I think until I write it down."

Nobody said finding new clients was going to be easy. But it can be done. Many other successful agency owners have blazed the trail. The next chapter tells you how to follow the path.

Marketing With A Bookism

AN AGENCY WITHOUT A BOOK IS LIKE A MOVIE THEATER WITHOUT A MARQUEE.

"When it comes to online marketing, I'm puzzled."

2

How To Find New Clients With A Book

Research has proven there is a better way. There is a proven process for marketing with integrity and getting up to 400 percent to 2,000 percent return on your marketing investment. I invented the Marketing With A Book Model, and many successful agencies use it to get more right-fit clients than they can handle. Some have made millions of dollars in the process. (For a look at the model, see appendix A.)

I will never forget the day I met agency owner Lisa Apolinski. She got me to agree to meet her for a thirty-minute cup of coffee and I stayed for three hours. (Lisa later confided she "stalked me" all the way from Phoenix to San Diego and called to say she "just happened to be in town." I call this the "I just happen to be in Kalamazoo strategy," which was taught to me by an agency owner and author who used the strategy to grow his firm into the Inc. 500 list of fastest-growing privately held firms. I have used the strat egy many times for my company.)

Lisa was a refugee from an international corporation who left when they would not listen to her ideas. She had side-hustle clients who did listen, and they started making serious money. So, she quit corporate life to form her own digital advertising agency, 3 Dog Write.

When we met for coffee, I found out she had already done the challenging work of getting her house in order, and now she wanted to have more impact and influence. "I want to double my revenues in three years and only work with Fortune 500 companies," she told me. At the time she had zero Fortune 500 clients.

"You can do that, Lisa, but it is not going to be easy," I told her. "You need to become a thought leader, and that means typing and talking. You need to gain credibility by writing books and speaking to important audiences."

Lisa was not sure how, and I told her if she supplied great insights for Fortune 500 companies, I would help her with the how.

Lisa went on to author three books in four years on digital marketing: *Weathering The Digital Storm* (2019), *Persuade With A Digital Content Story!* (2020), and *Gain Market Share In A Zombie Apocalypse* (2022). She is working on a fourth.

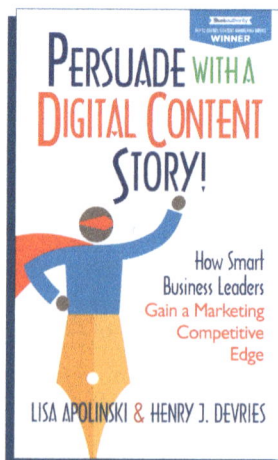

Cover design by Joni McPherson

She put the books in the hands of Fortune 500 marketing execs and CEOs, plus people who could publicize the book. As a result, she was written up in Forbes.com and invited to speak at prestigious places like a bank conference for HSBC Holdings, numerous podcasts, conferences, and even live on Australian television.

But she did not double her revenues in three years. She tripled her revenues and now works with household name brands such as one of the top five banks, one of the top five wealth management and financial services firms, and a billion-dollar Japanese electronics organization.

"Now I limit the number of Fortune 500 companies I work with because I want being a client of 3 Dog Write to be like joining an exclusive club," says Lisa.

Lisa gained more credibility, more impact, and more right-fit clients by typing and talking like a thought leader.

Testimony From Other Agency Owners

Want social proof? Here are what some other agency own-ers and high-end marketing consultants have to say:

> "The book is a tremendous support to my digital agency, Intuitive Websites, and has helped us grow to over $2 million in annual revenues," Thomas Young, agency owner of Intuitive Websites and author of *Winning the Website War*.

> "I set myself apart from the competition and built a multimillion-dollar firm, and credit the books with helping create $9 million in revenue," Tom

I SET MYSELF APART FROM THE COMPETITION AND BUILT A MULTIMILLION-DOLLAR FIRM, AND CREDIT THE BOOKS WITH HELPING CREATE $9 MILLION IN REVENUE

Searcy, agency owner of Hunt Big Sales and coauthor of *Whale Hunting* and *How to Close a Deal Like Warren Buffett.*

"I have made more than $280,000 a year as an author, speaker, and consultant. For over twenty years I wanted to write a book, but it was more of a wish than anything because I didn't know where or how to start," Penny Reed, marketing consultant and author of *Growing Your Dental Business.*

"I met Henry DeVries when he conducted a 'Growing Your Agency' workshop for our local PRSA [Public Relations Society of America] chapter. He shared one small idea that created a revenue stream for me of tens of thousands of dollars in that year alone. It was a million-dollar idea because it has resulted in more than that for my agency's revenues," Marisa Vallbona, APR, Fellow PRSA, agency owner of CIM Inc. PR.

Traditional Publishing Versus Indie Publishing Versus Self-Publishing: Which Is Best?

As an author I have published with traditional publishers, indie publishers, and I have self-published. Each has a place.

A brand name traditional publisher that pays you an advance on royalties, such as McGraw-Hill or Penguin, can boost credibility for an agency owner. One author I helped always is sure to name-drop that her book is from Stanford University Press.

The trick to getting such a traditional deal is the author must write a proposal that convinces the publisher that it cannot lose this book because the author has a platform and is going to work tirelessly to promote the book. Brand name publishers want to know that the author can sell ten thousand copies of a book a year.

But there are tens of thousands of publishers in the United States. If an author is with a traditional publisher that no one has heard of, there is no brand equity there. Some traditional publishing companies will offer to publish but with no advance on royalties, because they know the author will sell thousands of books.

Self-publishing had a bigger stigma before the digital age, but two technological advances were game changers: print-on-demand publishing and Amazon.com. With print-on-demand there no longer was the economy of scale needed to print thousands of books to get a low printing cost. With Amazon and other online retailers, there was no need to have a sales force that got the book into bookstores so the public could buy.

Indie publishing is really a hybrid between traditional publishing and self-publishing. Like indie films or indie music, the creator of the content owns the product and hires professionals to assist them to produce a quality product. Authors benefit from higher royalties and much lower author costs of books.

How Do I Choose
The Right Publisher For Me?

UNDER NO CIRCUMSTANCES SHOULD AN AUTHOR SAY HIS OR HER WORK IS SELF-PUBLISHED BECAUSE YOU WILL HAVE THE STIGMA ATTACHED TO SELF-PUBLISHED AUTHORS

For the author that has a platform (which means people who follow their work through social media or attending speeches), the best options are traditional publishing or indie publishing. There are pros and cons for each approach.

For the author that is still building a platform, the choice is clearer: indie publishing. Even if the author chooses self-publishing, the key is to make it look like indie publishing. Under no circumstances should an author say his or her work is self-published because you will have the stigma attached to self-published authors. And please, be sure to understand doing a digital-only book on the cheap is not going to give you the credibility and impact of a real printed book that prospects can actually hold in their hands.

How To Grow Your Platform To Land A Book Deal

A book deal is an agreement between a traditional royalty-based publisher and an author, by which the author agrees to write a book or a certain number of books to be published by the publisher.

Book deals for nonfiction business authors are getting increasingly rare.

If you want to get published by a big-name traditional publisher like Simon & Schuster or McGraw-Hill, you are going to need an author's platform. Editors at the big publishing houses in New York City tell me they don't want to look at a book proposal for an author unless that author has a great platform. Agents don't want to talk to you unless you have a great platform.

So, what the heck is that?

Platform is a catchphrase in the publishing world. It means you could reach out to an audience right now. It means you are the kind of author who could easily sell ten thousand or more copies in year one.

If you do not have a platform, you need a terrific plan on how you will build it soon.

Here are some elements:

Public speaking. You are regularly booked as a speaker.

Popular blog. You blog and people read it.

Podcast. You have fans who regularly listen to your podcasts.

Opt-in email list. You have a large list of people who regularly receive your email tips or articles.

15

YouTube. You have a significant YouTube subscriber list.

Business. You have an existing business with a big client or customer list of people who will buy your books.

If you want to attract high-paying clients, you need to be on YouTube.

If you are like me, you are going to YouTube as much as you are going to Google to search for answers.

Google is OK with that since they own YouTube.

To build platform, provide links to your live speaking engagements. This will help readers get more information about you in action. Media appearances are another major source of videos that build platform.

Indie Publishing Versus Self-Publishing: An Honest Comparison

Publishing a book is like building a house. Self-publishing is like being your own general contractor who must hire and manage all the subcontractors. Indie publishing is hiring a general contractor who already has an experienced and vetted team of subcontractors ready to go.

So, the choice is cobbling together your own team to publish a book or hiring an experienced team with a process to ensure success. There are many nitty-gritty details that go into publishing a book that represents you well.

As a self-published author, you'll need to hire a number of professionals to get your book ready to sell. If you work with a publisher, they will take most of these tasks off your plate. Either way, remember, the author is always responsible for marketing the book. This is true with traditional publishing, indie publishing, and self-publishing.

If you are a do-it-yourselfer, self-publishing may be for you. If all goes right, you can spend less money. However, mistakes can be costly, and you do not know what you do not know.

With self-publishing you get a bigger share of the royalties and the lowest author price on the book. With an indie-published book, you get the major share of the royalties, and the hope is with their help you will sell more books and make more money overall.

But please, if you go the self-publishing route, do not say your book is self-published. That is a marketing kiss of death. Instead, create a publishing house name and make the book appear as if it were published by a third party. This is marketing advice, not legal advice.

My Mess-To-Success Story

Before you take a guided tour, you should meet the tour guide.

Once upon a time, my business coach, Gary Hawk, took me to lunch at a Chinese restaurant and asked me four questions that changed my life.

First, he wanted to know what the exit strategy was for my San Diego marketing communications agency. Previously I had helped grow someone else's advertising agency, doubling revenues and landing us in the *Ad Age* 500 (now termed the Ad Age Agency Report rankings). The agency owner wanted to retire at fifty-five years of age and offered to sell the agency to me in what she called a "sweetheart deal." Upon close review I realized it was a sweetheart deal *for her* and indentured servitude for me. I walked away to form my own agency.

"So, what's the exit strategy?" Gary asked.

"Well, Gary, after I grow my firm for ten more years and have it running like a top, I am turning it over to a strategic buyer, and then I will teach agency owners how to attract clients," I said. "My wife and I are going to retire to a college town and spend our life surrounded by trees and water."

His second question was, "How would you do that?"

I excitedly told him I would write books, make speeches, put on conferences, and teach at a university. "There are so many agency owners that are great at what they do," I said, "but no one has ever taught them the science of attracting new clients. I have cracked the code."

Gary said, "You sound very passionate." I assured him I was. He then asked his third question. "Why are you waiting ten years to follow your passion?"

Don't you hate gut-check questions like that? Naturally, that question stumped me because my thoughts were on my obligations, clients, and employees. I described them as "the wolf at my door." In truth, I later discovered it was my own fear of failure.

Gary's fourth question helped me process: "How could you get started right now in a small way?"

"I can send invitations for a free monthly lunch seminar in my office," I ventured. "The turkey sandwiches would be on me, and I'd share with agency owners the science of finding clients."

My first free lunch-and-learn seminar was the very next month. The invitations were in the mail when the terrorist attack of September 11, 2001, took place in New York, Pennsylvania, and Washington, DC.

Later that horrible month, much to my surprise, agency owners and marketing consultants showed up for my lunch seminar. After I explained my theories, the attendees asked how much I'd charge to be their coach. Soon they asked me to write books for them and teach them to give speeches that attract clients. Meanwhile, while five of the top ten agencies in San Diego went out of business, my work helping agency owners and consultants to attract clients took over my business.

We renamed our company the New Client Marketing Institute. Over the next eight years, we invested $2 million in scientifically researching how to attract right-fit clients (that is now up to $5 million). We even tied in with the Harvard Business School. My research revealed a proven way for

MY RESEARCH REVEALED A PROVEN WAY FOR THE ABC (AGENCY OWNERS, BUSINESS COACHES, AND CONSULTANTS) TO OBTAIN A MARKETING RETURN-ON-INVESTMENT OF 400 PERCENT TO 2,000 PERCENT

the ABC (agency owners, business coaches, and consultants) to obtain a marketing return-on-investment of 400 percent to 2,000 percent. Since then, I've ghostwritten or edited more than three hundred business books and authored seventeen of my own.

These days, I annually speak to thousands of agency owners and consultants, teaching them writing and speaking strategies to attract high-paying clients and how to persuade with a story. In addition to running the New Client Marketing Institute, in 2007, I accepted an appointment as assistant dean for continuing education at UC San Diego, my alma mater, a campus located in a 1,200-acre grove of trees overlooking the Pacific Ocean. My wife was offered a position as a business manager for a large research center at the university.

College town. Trees. Water. My wife and me. Yup, the vision all came true.

While I loved my work at the university, I loved my fellow agency owners more. In 2014, my quest took a new turn. I launched Indie Books International. Agency owners and consultants turn to us for help with the preparation, publication, and promotion of a book that grows their business, puts money in the bank, and helps them make the difference they want to make. Indie Books International was founded by two best-selling authors: Mark LeBlanc and me. We educate agency owners that the publication of the book is the starting line, not the finish line.

In Part II, let me share some insights on how you can successfully run the race. But first let's explore the crossroads we now find ourselves.

Marketing With A Bookism

START WRITING NO MATTER WHAT. PERFECTION IS THE ENEMY OF DONE, AND DONE IS BETTER THAN PERFECT.

3

Welcome To The Renaissance: Now Innovate Or Die

Agencies are on the cusp of a season of opportunity that the world has not seen in a long time. That was the message marketing expert Drew McLellan delivered to more than 225 marketing agency leaders at the Build A Better Agency Summit in May 2022 in Chicago.

"Historians, business leaders, and our own experience would suggest that we're entering into an era like the Great Renaissance," said McLellan. "The question is: what part will we play? Are we the leaders who will get challenged and replaced, or are we the innovators that will create new business models and drive innovation and creativity?"

The choice is a stark one of fantastic opportunity and significant risk.

"We're at the beginning of another renaissance," said McLellan. "After every major world event—usually a bad one, like the bubonic plague or World War II—there was a rebirth. A time of incredible innovation, creativity, and an economic boom."

McLellan has worked in advertising for more than twenty-five years and started his own agency, McLellan

ARE WE THE LEADERS WHO WILL GET CHALLENGED AND REPLACED, OR ARE WE THE INNOVATORS THAT WILL CREATE NEW BUSINESS MODELS AND DRIVE INNOVATION AND CREATIVITY?

Marketing Group, in 1995, after five years with Young & Rubicam. He also owns and operates the summit's presenter, Agency Management Institute (AMI), which is a consultancy for small to mid-sized agencies that has been helping agency owners grow since the early 1990s.

His first book, 99.3 Random Acts of Marketing, was published in 2003. He is a coauthor of the 2020 book Sell with Authority.[6]

McLellan told the crowd: "See if this sounds familiar. People are put in a circumstance both out of their control and far beyond what they could have possibly imagined. Everything changes rapidly and with little warning. In each of the events that led to a renaissance, our very existence was threatened. We faced our own mortality. We lost loved ones."

Though the plague was as grim as it sounds, there was an unseen benefit. According to McLellan, the plague helped create the conditions necessary for the greatest post-pandemic recovery of all time—the Great Renaissance.

"Priorities changed and new business models emerged," said McLellan. "Necessity inspired a whole new level of innovation and creativity."

He noted the Renaissance became known for its art, music, and architecture. The period is commonly associated with Michelangelo's Sistine Chapel, his majestic statue of

David, Gutenberg's printing press, and Leonardo da Vinci's Mona Lisa.

"But the Renaissance also laid the foundation for the very fabric of our modern society: capitalism," said McLellan. "As feudalism died along with the plague, individual wealth took its place. Merchants and commerce, banking, property investments, and advances in science propelled people forward and our corporate roots began to grow."

This was a moment in time when they had to reinvent. They had to try new things. They had to do what had never been done before. Sounds familiar, doesn't it?

The crisis was the catalyst for dramatic change, creativity, and the birth of many new and lasting innovations.

"Following World War II, we also experienced a renaissance," noted McLellan. Wages were 50 percent higher than they were five years prior and unemployment was completely eliminated. Shipyards cut the time it took to build a ship from 365 days to less than a week. The flu vaccine was invented, as was the first modern computer.

McClellan's motto for the Build A Better Agency Summit is: "We grow faster and learn better when we learn together."

Marketing With A Bookism

THERE ARE TWO REASONS FOR AN AGENCY OWNER TO WRITE A BOOK: ONE, SO YOU BECOME AN EXPERT, AND TWO, SO YOU CAN SPEAK MORE TO PROVE IT.

PART II

The How

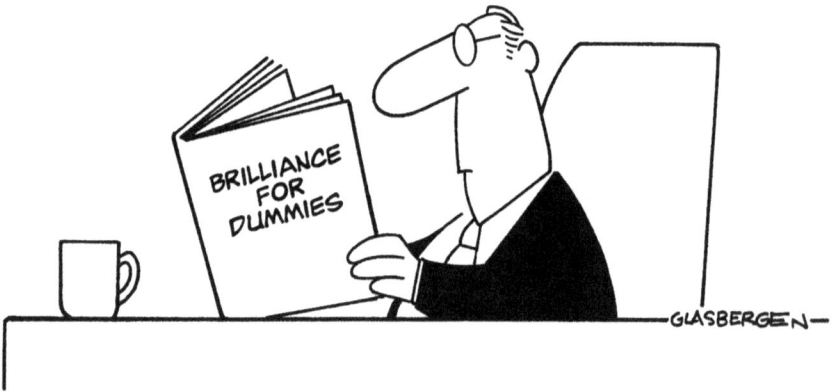

4

Hype, Not Help

What is the secret of attracting high-paying clients?

"Being relentlessly helpful," says Stephen Woessner, co-author with Drew McLellan of the book *Sell with Authority*.

Woessner says research gives you something helpful to say. But where and how deep are you willing to plant your flag of authority?

"When you think about how best to create your cornerstone content, don't think about what's trendy," says Woessner. "Instead, focus on what will provide the most value to your audience and what aligns best with the gifts and talents of you and your team."

Woessner runs an agency called Predictive ROI. For more than twenty-five years he has worked with agencies, consultants, and coaches to fill their sales pipelines with right-fit clients. He is an advocate of creating what he terms *cornerstone content* to create a depth of knowledge and point-of-view that cannot be easily replicated.

To market like a thought leader, it all comes down to research and then talking or typing.

"Maybe you talk it out by hosting a podcast and interviewing people or creating a valuable YouTube video series consistently to share with your audience," says Woessner.

"Perhaps you want to build your reputation by being a keynote speaker."

Or maybe writing is more your thing.

"You could write a book, post a valuable blog series, create a quarterly e-Book series that goes deep into your niche, or perhaps an annual research series that knits back into the e-Books," says Woessner.

Woessner says creating cornerstone content is where many agencies, strategic consultants, and business coaches miss the mark when it comes to content strategy.

"We get overwhelmed at the thought of having to create content on a consistent basis, so we err on the side of deciding to make a lot of little pieces of content as opposed to starting with something substantial," says Woessner. "For some reason, writing fifty blog posts seems less daunting than one research project a year or writing a book every couple of years."

Woessner says you build a dependable sales pipeline with thought leadership research, a strategy I typically call proprietary client research, which I learned from the writings of David Maister.

"Clients today are bombarded with articles, speeches, and seminars that contain generalities and do not distinguish the author

CLIENTS TODAY ARE BOMBARDED WITH ARTICLES, SPEECHES, AND SEMINARS THAT CONTAIN GENERALITIES AND DO NOT DISTINGUISH THE AUTHOR OR PRESENTER FROM ANY OF HIS OR HER COMPETENT COMPETITORS

or presenter from any of his or her competent competitors," said former Harvard Business School professor Maister.

In his classic 1997 book *Managing the Professional Service Firm*, Maister explained how to prove that you have something to offer that your competitors do not.

By conducting proprietary research, you obtain specific information that prospective clients can't find elsewhere. Typically, this is about how they compare to their peers. The foundation of selling with authority is to give away cornerstone content through talking and typing, which demonstrates to the client niche you target that you have the expertise to help them.

"Creating cornerstone content is the key to stepping into your rightful position of being a thought leader, someone with authority," says Woessner.

Research, Not Rehash

"You don't have to wait until you can pull off a major new research study to start building your thought leadership with research," says Susan Baier of Audience Audit. "Even small, simple approaches can be a great start."

Baier Has more than thirty years of experience in audience-based marketing strategy, including product and brand management, market research, and strategic planning, both agency-side and client-side. She earned an MBA in entrepreneurship and marketing and has served in senior positions at Fortune 100 and Fortune 500 companies in addition to marketing agencies.

"If you collect information from your customers, you can probably build thought leadership content from data you already have," says Baier. "Many of our agency clients working on thought leadership research worry that they don't have a strong niche. Many do—they're just not thinking about niche the way I think they should."

Make Generosity Your Brand

If you are an agency principal who wants to find new clients on a smooth and sustainable basis, generosity is the killer strategy.

Ad agency founder Jason Harris concurs.

"The person who only comes around when it is obvious that they need or want something from you, is not someone that earns our trust," says Harris. "People like that suck the life out of us. When their name appears in our inbox, our day automatically gets a little more meh and we roll our eyes."

Harris cofounded and is CEO of award-winning creative advertising agency Mekanism; cofounder of Creative Alliance; and wrote the national bestseller, *The Soulful Art of Persuasion*. Harris works with prominent companies such as Peloton, Ben & Jerry's, Jose Cuervo, Alaska Airlines, and Charles Schwab, as well as others.

"On the other hand, an individual who leaves you just slightly better off every time you encounter him or her is precisely the person who is likely to get your attention when they need or want something from you," says Harris. "So how do you become the right type of person? By being generous by nature."

Harris says being generous doesn't come naturally to some people. But if you commit to practicing generosity in every interaction, you'll find that generosity will become habitual.

"So, try this: every time you interact with someone—whether it's at a business meeting, virtual call, reconnecting with friends—try to give something away," says Harris. "Treat all of your encounters as a chance to flex your generosity muscles."

A common misconception about generosity: being generous translates to solely money or gifts. However, covering costs might be the least memorable thing you can give away. He says if you enter every encounter thinking, "What can I contribute? How can I give away something valuable?" the answer usually falls into a few basic categories: time, attention, or counsel.

When it comes to finding new clients, the options of time, attention, or counsel play out in various forms. In my view, there are many ways to be generous with prospective clients. You can give away white papers, research study results, monographs, how-to articles, practical tips, and case studies. You share these by typing and talking—either in written form or the spoken word.

Talking is more important than typing. Prospects are impacted more when they experience you through podcast appearances, speeches, and workshops you host.

WHEN IT COMES TO FINDING NEW CLIENTS, THE OPTIONS OF TIME, ATTENTION, OR COUNSEL PLAY OUT IN VARIOUS FORMS

"Go into key interactions thinking about what, if anything, you can contribute or what's being asked of you," says Harris. "Is this an opportunity to offer a useful piece of information or a connection? Or does the situation call for a bit of honest feedback? It could be that the person you've connected with would appreciate a copy of a book you just read or an article that relates to their situation. Don't feel the need to know ahead of time what the right response will be in each instance; once you begin seeing interactions as opportunities to give stuff away, the answer usually comes into focus, and you can always listen to your gut."

How does this pay off in terms of business development? It certainly has helped Harris succeed.

Under his leadership, Mekanism was named Independent Agency of the Year by The Drum and ranked by the Effie Index as a Top Ten Most Effective Independent Agency in the United States. Harris was also named 2021 CEO of the Year by The Drum, a recipient of the 4A's 100 People Who Make Advertising Great, and a 2020 Campaign US 40 Over 40 honoree for his noteworthy contributions to the advertising and marketing industry. His methods are studied in cases at Harvard Business School.

"The rule of reciprocity will come back to you tenfold and you will be known as a kind and generous soul," says Harris.

Where We Are Going

If you are the kind of reader who skips to the end or can't wait to get started, I recommend you skip to appendix B, which outlines my Book BluePrint Process. If you want more details on the how, I recommend you proceed to the next chapters in Part II, which spell out how to master this in detail.

Marketing With A Bookism

TO PARAPHRASE COMIC GENIUS GROUCHO MARX, OUTSIDE OF A DOG, A BOOK IS AN AGENCY OWNER'S BEST FRIEND. INSIDE OF A DOG IT IS TOO DARK TO READ.

5

Riches In Niches

To attract high-paying clients, agency owners must be clear on their ideal prospects.

Once I asked an attorney what kind of law he practiced. He replied: "Rent law. Any law that pays the rent."

Before an agency owner can begin to easily generate solid client leads, they need to clearly define their target prospect.

The search begins with this question: What problem do you solve and for whom?

Here are some niche examples:

Accountants for social enterprises: CPAs who work with leaders of nonprofit organizations to make sure they do not run afoul of the IRS 501(c) tax codes.

Family business consultants: Consultants who work with owners of multimillion-dollar family businesses who do not know how to exit so they can afford to retire.

Family law attorneys: Lawyers who help couples who want an amicable divorce and do not want a judge to force them to liquidate assets.

Financial advisors: Trusted advisors who work with people who do not know if they will have enough money to last after they quit working.

AGENCY OWNERS ALSO MUST FIND TARGET CLIENTS THAT CAN AFFORD TO PAY WHAT YOU WANT TO CHARGE

Healthcare providers: Medical professionals helping people enjoy life and thrive.

Home builders: Developers who create homes for families.

Some say there are only three flavors of problems: money, health, and love. However, it is the specifics that create powerful business development.

But a target market with a problem is not enough. Agency owners also must find target clients that can afford to pay what you want to charge.

Finding a niche target market takes time, effort, and a dedication many agency owners do not know how to give.

In researching a target market, here are ten filter questions to ponder, in the following order:

1. **Are you interested in solving the problems this group has?** If their problems do not energize you, that should be a nonstarter.

2. **Have you worked with any already?** Targeting prospects in a market you have never worked with is possible, but not probable. Prospects want a successful track record.

3. **Can they afford you?** Money isn't everything, but it is certainly one important thing.

4. **Are they willing to pay more for better service?** There is no winning the low-price provider game. You cash bigger checks by providing better service to those willing to pay for it.

WRITER   COPYWRITER

5. Do they already know they need an agency like you? If you must educate the prospect that they need an agency like yours, then you are waging an uphill battle.

6. Are they numerous? One of my clients goes fishing. He says: "If you want to catch catfish, go to a fishing hole where the catfish are. The more catfish there are, the better the fishing will be. That's just math." In his brilliant book *The Business of Expertise*, Nashville-based business consultant David C. Baker advises there should be two- to ten-thousand prospects.[7]

7. Do you have only a few real competitors? If this is an attractive market, then it will attract other agencies. Even if you discover and create a new market, others will find it too. The trick is to offer a unique problem-solving process, which you document and trademark. Clients like process and find a proprietary process that you value as intellectual property as differentiating when they choose who to hire.

8. Can you find them easily enough through lists and associations? Demographics matter. You should be able to define with numbers your target market. Psychographics are well and good, but it's hard to find a list.

9. Can you find a target-rich environment where they gather? Go again to the fishing hole metaphor. If you prefer, what is their watering hole? What do they read and what do they attend? You can Google that stuff (I know, I used a noun as a verb).

10. Will some make marquee clients, advocates, and references? This might be a hush-hush group that never wants it known that you helped them. That will make it hard to demonstrate a successful track record in your testimonials.

Bottom line: The more quality thinking you do up front, the easier your business development will be.

Marketing With A Bookism

WHEN SOMEONE SAYS, "I HAVE YOUR BOOK," THAT IS CODE FOR, "SOMEDAY I MIGHT READ IT."

"*That pill they advertise all the time on TV. I'm not sure what it is, but I want it!*"

6

Think Like A Thought Leader

Are you thinking about becoming a thought leader?

If you want to attract high-paying clients by marketing like a thought leader, you must commit to becoming an expert. Especially if your expertise is in a subject many think of as taboo.

Consider the career of Rachel Braun Scherl, a thought leader in women's sexual health and wellness. A self-described "vagipreneur," Scherl is a market-maker in the multibillion-dollar global women's sexual health subsector.

"Building expertise in an area requires constant learning, innovative thinking, building partnerships, and the willingness to face challenges," says Scherl. "This is especially true in women's sexual and reproductive health, where entrepreneurs are creating solutions,

> BUILDING EXPERTISE IN AN AREA REQUIRES CONSTANT LEARNING, INNOVATIVE THINKING, BUILDING PARTNERSHIPS, AND THE WILLINGNESS TO FACE CHALLENGES

creating conversations, and driving growth."

Scherl spends a great deal of time speaking publicly, loudly, and passionately, in an effort to drive the conversation around the business of female health and sexual pleasure.

After a successful career in corporate America, Scherl became an entrepreneur because she wanted to be more in control of her financial future. She cofounded SPARK with her longtime business partner, Mary Wallace Jaensch. Her international client roster includes multiple divisions of Johnson & Johnson, Allergan, Pfizer, Merck, Bayer, and more. Scherl and I met when I helped her publish a book about profiting from the coming surge of women's sexual health and wellness, *Orgasmic Leadership*. The title was too provocative for many, and that was the point she was trying to make.

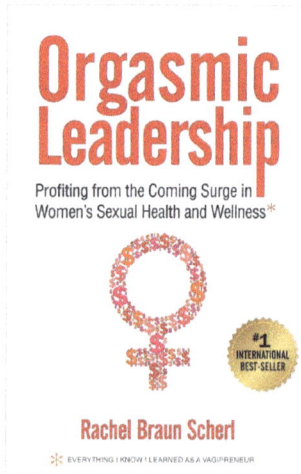

Cover design by Joni McPherson

"The growing awareness of the 'size of the prize' has led to a boom in the founding of companies that meet a broad range of needs out of medical, gynecological, sexual, and reproductive necessity," says Scherl. "I am passionate about reframing entrenched beliefs about women's sexuality, with an important emphasis on creating conversations. Without a vocabulary, the conversation and progress would be stalled before they start."

Scherl feels strongly that today's industry leaders need a language for the complexity of female sexuality to destigmatize pressing health and aging concerns for women.

"With that common vocabulary, companies can grow businesses in historically taboo areas," says Scherl. "The first step of building that expertise is an obsession with the subject matter—and who better to be at the helm of their own health than women?"

She preaches that entrepreneurs, academics, health care professionals, and investors are driving the efforts to bring innovative technology to market, develop better solutions for a wide range of sexual and reproductive health concerns, and create the companies to deliver on those needs.

"As the needs are complex, the solutions must be thoughtful, accessible, and useful, providing information, customization, education, and often immediate gratification," says Scherl. "Interestingly, the education piece provided by companies is often filling a gap left by the current state, or lack thereof, of sex education."

A thought leader needs to write and speak, and it helps to win awards. Scherl is the recipient of numerous business awards: SmartCEO's BRAVA Awards honoring top female CEOs, Top Twenty-Five Entrepreneurs in New Jersey, and Best Fifty Women in Business by NJBiz.

Thought leaders need to get involved and collaborate. Scherl is a board member of the Center for Entrepreneurship and Innovation for Fuqua School of Business at Duke University and serves on the boards of multiple women's health and wellness companies.

"I have been a proud contributor/participant in this space, with a laser-like focus on the intersection of women's health and businesses responding to them," says Scherl. "By driving growth with companies—large and small, established and developing—I have the frequent opportunity to collaborate with investors, inventors, entrepreneurs, conference leads, researchers, academics, and health care practitioners."

In addition to seeing increased investment in women's sexual health and wellness, she has observed a spike in conversations regarding all aspects of women's health, including pleasure, which she says is long overdue.

"Today companies are talking about all aspects of women's health, from menstruation to menopause," says Scherl.

Marketing With A Bookism

IF YOUR BOOK TELLS REAL TRUTH, IT WILL MAKE TURNSTILES TURN AND CASH REGISTERS RING.

7

Prospects Relate To Eight Great Stories

Every agency book should tell a story.

There are eight great meta stories that humans want to hear repeatedly. What type of story are you telling?

In other words, there are eight basic story structures a book can take, based on the classic eight structures that all "stories" follow. This is based on *The Seven Basic Plots: Why We Tell Stories*, a 2004 book by British journalist Christopher Booker, a Jungian-influenced analysis of stories and their psychological meaning.[8] (Booker said an eighth was added 150 years ago with the mystery.)

I compared Booker's eight categories and discovered the same story structure rules apply to the greatest business nonfiction books of all time. Here are the eight categories:

Monster. A terrifying, all-powerful, life-threatening monster whom the hero must confront in a fight to the death. An example of this plot is seen in *Beowulf, Jaws, Jack and the Beanstalk*, and *Dracula*. Most business books follow this plot. There is some monster problem in the workplace, and this is how you attack it. Business book examples: *Slay the E-Mail Monster, The*

THE BUSINESS BOOKS IN THIS CATEGORY DISCUSS HOW SOMEONE RAISED THEMSELVES UP FROM NOTHING TO SUCCESS, A TYPICAL RAGS-TO-RICHES STORY

E-Myth Revisited, Whale Hunters, Growing Your Business.

Underdog. Someone who has seemed to the world quite commonplace is shown to have been hiding a second, more exceptional self within. Think *The Ugly Duckling, Cinderella, Jane Eyre, Rudy,* and Clark Kent (*Superman*). The business books in this category discuss how someone raised themselves up from nothing to success, a typical rags-to-riches story. One of my early favorites was *Up from Slavery* by Booker T. Washington. Business book examples: *Moneyball, Up the Organization, Grinding It Out.*

Quest. From the moment the hero or heroine learns of the priceless goal, he or she sets out on a hazardous journey to reach it. Examples are seen in *The Odyssey, The Count of Monte Cristo,* and *Raiders of the Lost Ark.* Business book examples: *The HP Way, In Search of Excellence, The One Minute Manager, How to Win Friends and Influence People, How to Close a Deal Like Warren Buffett, Never Be the Same.*

Escape. The hero or heroine and a few companions travel out of familiar surroundings into another world completely cut off from the first. While it is at first wonderful, there is a sense of increasing peril. After a dramatic escape, they return to the familiar world where they began. *Alice in Wonderland* and *The Time Machine* are obvious examples, but *The Wizard of Oz* and *Gone with the Wind* also embody this basic plotline. Business book examples: *The Prodigal Executive*, *The Innovator's Dilemma*.

Comedy. Think of the movies *Wedding Crashers*, *Tootsie*, and *Some Like It Hot*. Following a general chaos of misunderstanding, the characters tie themselves and each other into a knot that seems almost unbearable; however, to universal relief, everyone and everything gets sorted out, bringing about a happy conclusion. This is about solving an idea with a wacky idea. Shakespeare's comedies come to mind, as do Jane Austen's novels like *Sense and Sensibility*. Business book examples: *2030: The Real Story of What Happens to America*, *A Whack on the Side of the Head*, *Losing My Virginity*, *Swim with the Sharks without Being Eaten Alive*.

Tragedy. This is about solving a problem by going against the laws of nature, society, or God. A character through some flaw or lack of self-understanding is increasingly drawn into a fatal course of action that leads inexorably to disaster. *King Lear*, *Othello*, *The Godfather*, *Madame Bovary*, *The Picture of Dorian Gray*, *Breaking Bad*, *Scarface*, and *Bonnie and Clyde*—all flagrantly tragic. Business book examples: *Too Big to Fail*, *Barbarians at the Gate*, *Liar's Poker*.

Rebirth. There is a mounting sense of threat as a dark force approaches the hero until it emerges completely, holding the hero in its deadly grip. Only after a time, when the dark force has triumphed, does the reversal take place. The hero is redeemed, usually through the life-giving power of love. Many fairy tales take this shape—also, works like *Silas Marner*, *Beauty and the Beast*, *A Christmas Carol*, and *It's a Wonderful Life*. Business book examples: *Out of the Crisis*, *Seabiscuit* (note from author: my editor hates this example, but I grew up in the horse racing business).

Mystery. This appeared from the time of Edgar Allan Poe. From Sherlock Holmes to Agatha Christie to *CSI: Miami*, the plot that involves solving a riddle has gained immense popularity in the last 150 years. Business book examples: *Good to Great*, *Think and Grow Rich*, *The Secret*, *Cracking the Personality Code*.

> **Marketing With A Bookism**
> HOLLYWOOD ONLY MAKES EIGHT MOVIES, AND IT IS A $600 BILLION A YEAR INDUSTRY.

8

Prospects Love Process

Creating your memorable methodology is a wonderful place to start to become an agency that attracts high-paying clients.

This is the best way to position yourself as a trusted authority to your ideal prospects.

Scott Cantrell, who says his clients have generated more than $100 million of additional revenues by becoming trusted authorities, believes the answer comes down to three words: "Insight inspires influence."

To help clients have more influence and insight, Cantrell and his firm Smart Solutions Media work with business owners and professionals who want to attract high-value prospects and acquire more profitable clients by positioning themselves as trusted authorities.

"If you want to have a position of preeminence and become a trusted authority, then you must

AGENCY OWNERS WHO CONSISTENTLY PROVIDE INSIGHT TO THE MARKETPLACE AFFIRM THE NEED (AND DESIRE) TO HEAR FROM THEM, FOLLOW THEM, LEARN FROM THEM, AND WORK WITH THEM

share your insights, and they must be clear, compelling, and consistent," says Cantrell. Agency owners who consistently provide insight to the marketplace affirm the need (and desire) to hear from them, follow them, learn from them, and work with them.

Deliver Memorable Methodology

"Not your product, service, or solution, but your methodology is your single most sustainable competitive advantage. Develop and name your own approach. Next, create a short assessment process for potential clients that naturally leads them to two conclusions: they need help and you're the one to provide that help," says Cantrell.

What Cantrell calls memorable methodology I call proprietary process. Based on my interviews with successful client rainmakers, it is a game changer.

David C. Baker[9], Nashville-based business consultant and author, says one of the most common mistakes an agency can make is not having a defined, proprietary process. Writing in his newsletter *Persuading* (available through his website, recourses.com), Baker highlights several reasons why a memorable methodology is important.

PROCESS IS DIFFERENTIATING, HIGHLIGHTING THE UNIQUENESS OF YOUR FIRM WITH A PROCESS THAT YOU OWN

"Process is differentiating, highlighting the uniqueness of your firm with a process that you own," says Baker. Other advantages he cites are that a process demonstrates your experience, makes your work less accidental and will even allow you to charge more. "Clients are always willing to pay more for packages than individual hours within a fee structure."

A great memorable methodology, however, is never a cookie-cutter industry standard lifted from a textbook. Instead, it codifies a firm's particular method of problem-solving, typically identifying and sequencing multiple steps that often take place in the same, defined order. The process name should be trademarked to show that you value this piece of intellectual property.

Prospects Find Process Comforting

If you want to find new clients, take a cue from a trusted advisor who regularly attracts seven-figure investors.

"Attracting ideal clients is more than a numbers game in today's world," says four-time author Brittany Anderson.

Anderson offers a proprietary trademarked planning process that focuses on dreaming to attract million-dollar investors. She says it is the intersection of where money and mindset meet.

"Some may say differentiation and a target niche is the secret to success," says Anderson. "While those things are important, the best client relationships are built out of impact and helping the person realize possibility for their future with the help of your services."

Like Anderson, you should create a trademarked way of solving client problems. Give the process a name and take the steps to trademark the process, which communicates this is a key part of your brand. Without a proprietary process, you are just a commodity.

Anderson, partner and president at Sweet Financial Partners, has coached hundreds of business owners and entrepreneurs.

"At face value, high net worth investors may be looking for creative tax planning strategies, investment vehicles that help them advance and preserve their wealth, and an advisor to lean on throughout the process," says Anderson. "What we have found they are actually searching for is a deeper purpose and meaning for their years of saving and accumulation."

All the money in the world doesn't matter when there isn't a clear intent for what it can do for the person's life and legacy.

"There is a massive shift occurring in the wealth advising and planning industry," says Anderson. "While basic investment management used to do the job for seven-, eight-, and nine-figure investors, which isn't the case anymore. We are at a time where thanks to advances in the medical field, people are living longer."

What does living longer have to do with investment strategies? Everything.

Anderson says health and longevity impact not only the numbers side of a person's plan, but also how they think about retirement in general. What used to be a ten- to fifteen-year slow-down period heading into retirement is now turning into a runway toward opportunity.

Therefore, her firm created its trademarked process called The Dream Architect. When you trademark your process, you communicate to prospects that this is important intellectual property that differentiates you from the average advisor.

"We believe that every person has the right to realize exponential possibility for their future," says Anderson. "What began as a four-step planning process has turned into a method of helping people to identify their values and change their mindset around the term 'returns.' We provide ample resources to help people pursue experiences they never thought possible. Our hope is that by helping others identify their *why* in retirement, people will live more fulfilled and longer retirements."

Bottom line: it pays to brand yourself with a proprietary, trademarked process.

Marketing With A Bookism
THE BEST AGENCY BOOKS ARE THE ONES THAT GET YOU HIRED.

"Yes, *we have* Chicken Soup For The Investor's Soul.
Do you want to pay cash or buy it on margin?"

9

Human Brains Are Hardwired For Stories

Do you want more high-paying clients? It pays to spin a good yarn.

Discoveries in neuroscience prove people make decisions based on emotion, not logic.[10] These are emotional times, and if you want to attract more high-paying clients you need to become a better business storyteller who reaches the emotion part of the brain.

Start by focusing on the worst part of the story.

"It's a surprise of sorts," says award-winning author Dave Lieber. "The best part of any story is the worst part. Don't skip through it."

Lieber, a certified professional speaker, is an expert at teaching storytelling in business. He shows individuals, businesses, and industries how to use stories to meet their goals.

"The low point of a good business story is the most important part. So why do you

THE LOW POINT OF A GOOD BUSINESS STORY IS THE MOST IMPORTANT PART. SO WHY DO YOU KEEP RUSHING THROUGH IT?

keep rushing through it?" asks Lieber.

Stories about clients you have helped solve a problem can establish your credibility in under two minutes.

"Every good story has a beginning, middle, and end," says Lieber. "Every good story has a hero and a villain. And most good stories have a happy ending that symbolizes accomplishment and offers an important lesson."

Lieber has honed his craft as the national-award-winning "Watchdog" columnist for the *Dallas Morning News*. (His fish-out-of-water stories about moving from the East Coast to Texas are solid gold.) We met when he spoke at a conference I hosted for new authors.

"But I've noticed that most business storytellers ignore the most important part of the story," says Lieber. "They fail to emphasize the low point, the worst part of the story for the hero—the problem that needs to be solved."

The author of nine books, Lieber is also a playwright with two plays on stage in Dallas-Fort Worth.

If the story shows it was easy for the hero, that is boring. Some business storytellers like to skip the middle struggle part of the story.

"Here's why that's a big mistake: we learn more from our failures and struggles than we do from our successes," says Lieber. "When the hero decides to take a giant step out of the low point and beat back the villain, we learn a tremendous amount of helpful information."

According to Lieber, when the low point is slighted and quickly passed over to get to the climactic ending, we lose learning opportunities.

"That's why as a writer, keynote speaker, and trainer I teach clients to dwell in the low point," says Lieber. "Live there in the story long enough for the audience to feel the

HUMAN BRAINS ARE HARDWIRED FOR STORIES

discomfort. Put the audience in the middle of the story. Make them feel some of the confusion, the difficulties, and the challenge of the low point."

When this is done properly, the journey from the low point to the climax is more emotional and memorable.

"By the ending, lessons are learned and not forgotten," says Lieber.

Welcome To The Story Wars

Attention is our most precious and rarest commodity if we want to attract high-paying clients.

The competition for the hearts, minds, and eyeballs of prospects grows ever more intense. Nobody knows precisely how many people have entered the independent thought leader/expert industry, but we do know each year brings a bigger crop of combatants to what Jonah Sachs famously calls "the story wars."

"The story wars are being waged all around us," writes Sachs in his book *Winning the Story Wars*. "These are the battles fought by companies, brands, causes, public figures, and individuals to be heard above the unprecedented noise of the post-broadcast, social-media-dominated era. Today, most brand messages and mass appeals for causes are drowned out before they even reach us."

What does this mean for those who want to attract clients as a thought leader/expert?

"In short, it's this: you can do all the marketing, sales training, and SEO-optimizing you want, but unless the story (the main idea or offer of help) at the heart of your small business is compelling, all your other activities constitute merely the opportunity to bore, confuse or annoy more people," says social media contrarian Ellen Melko Moore of Supertight Social Selling.

Melko Moore, formerly a faculty member at the University of Denver, is a social selling expert who specializes in LinkedIn, and has worked with hundreds of service-minded entrepreneurs to create compelling and powerful brands through remarkable content.

YOU CANNOT DECLARE YOURSELF A THOUGHT LEADER—YOU MUST EARN IT

Thought leaders are people who write and speak about a subject and are quoted by others. You cannot declare yourself a thought leader—you must earn it. Here are several ways Melko Moore advises wannabe thought leaders to improve their brands:

Feature Results. "Nothing sells quite as well as a tasty result," says Melko Moore. "Measurable results are a great story that should always be an important part of the story of a brand. For example, if you're a CEO coach who helped your CEO client sell his business for $70 million (instead of the $15 million he was told by market analysts that he could expect to receive), that's a story that will get locked and loaded in your prospects' minds. It's concrete, memorable, and proves that talking to Steve Brody (the CEO coach in question) would be a darn good idea."

Be Specific. "One of the fastest ways to change your story on LinkedIn is to choose a very specific target audience and design your profile, outreach, and content to educate that particular audience," says Melko Moore. "Let's say that you own a digital marketing agency working with women-owned businesses. Sharpen your focus on LinkedIn to position yourself as *the* digital marketing agency for women-owned law firms. Pursue this focus with consistency and discover you've quickly gone to the front of the line in this category."

Think Tighter. Melko Moore believes small business owners and solopreneurs who want to market as thought leaders are aware that a tighter target audience is a great *idea*, but most are extremely reluctant to make that change. They're too concerned about who they might be "ruling out." She says it's time to give more thought to who you're "ruling in."

"In the last three years, we've been using LinkedIn to test target audiences and messaging, and the results have been dynamic," says Melko Moore. "Many successful small business leaders will admit they're not getting huge results from their LinkedIn activity, so they're more willing to use the platform to test a potential position, without having to change their entire digital footprint until they see those improved results."

Marketing With A Bookism

THE BEST TIME FOR AN AUTHOR IS NOT WHEN THEY PUBLISH THEIR FIRST BOOK BUT WHEN THEY PUBLISH THEIR SECOND. THAT WAY, WHEN SOMEONE SAYS THEY WOULD LIKE TO READ YOUR BOOK, YOU CAN SAY, "OH, WHICH ONE?"

"Okay, let me come at this question a different way:
Does anybody here actually know how to sell anything?

10

Pain, Not Gain, To Make It Rain

If you are an agency owner who struggles with marketing, you are not alone. Many agency owners are tired of the rejection, frustration, and mystery of marketing.

There is a better way to attract clients: talk about avoiding pain, not about seeking a gain. In other words, lead with the negative. The secret is to turn their pain into your gain. Start by asking clients about their pains. Then gather information on how to solve those worries, frustrations, and concerns.

Let me ask you this (now be honest): Do you really understand the problems of your prospects and clients? Or do you just think you know? Make no doubt about it—the stakes are high. Wrong marketing messages will cost you potential clients and lead to more struggles and discouragement.

In my workshops when I say: "You make more money selling Vicodin than vitamins," somebody always quips: "What about selling Viagra?"

Viagra solves a pain. Trust me.

A Cool Tool For Probing Prospect Pain

WHAT'S THE SECRET TO CRAFTING A MARKETING MESSAGE THAT WILL MAXIMIZE YOUR ATTRACTION FACTOR? ASK THEM ABOUT THEIR PAINS

Here's how to become a new client magnet. Each group of prospects experiences its own unique frustrations and pains. What's the secret to crafting a marketing message that will maximize your attraction factor? Ask them (or have someone ask for you) about their pains. Start by asking a sample about their ideal business, and then segue into problems. Listen carefully to the exact words they use (you will want to mimic them in your marketing messages).

Chris Stiehl, a marketing research consultant, and my coauthor on *Pain Killer Marketing*, created this tool.[11] When you interview some current, past, and potential clients about the pains you solve, here are ten questions you should always ask:

1. Describe for me the "ideal" experience with a
_____
(your profession or line of consulting). How do most compare to this ideal?

2. Describe for me a recent time that the experience was less than ideal.

3. What are the three most important aspects of doing business with a_____?

4. If I said a _____
was an excellent value, what would that mean to you?

5. In what ways does dealing with a _____
cost you besides money (time, hassle, effort, etc.)?

6. What is the biggest pain about working with a
_____?

7. Would you recommend a _____
to a friend or colleague? Why, or why not?

8. How does working with a _____
help you make money?

9. What does a _____ do well?

10. If you had the opportunity to work with a
_____
again, would you? Why, or why not?

Marketing With A Bookism

READERS HAVE THE RIGHT NOT TO READ YOUR BOOK. IF YOU DON'T WRITE THE RIGHT BOOK, THEY WILL EXERCISE THAT RIGHT.

"In hindsight, I'd say my first mistake was letting my competitors advertise on my website."

11

Books Don't Promote Authors; Authors Promote Books

Never forget that books don't promote authors; authors promote books. An author who writes a book to promote their agency needs to shine the spotlight on the book in hopes of gaining buzz. Just publishing a book is not enough. Agency owners must work to see that people read and hear about the book.

When it comes to promotion, Minal Sampat is an immigrant who thinks big. At the age of twenty-eight, she launched her first marketing agency by breaking a Guinness World Record.

"In 2013, I launched my first marketing company by breaking a Guinness World Record, so that I could share my knowledge and experience with businesses looking to achieve their dreams," said Sampat. "With 1,530 participants, we broke the world record for the most simultaneous mouthwash swishers at one time. This event, Swish Away Breast Cancer, not only raised awareness for breast cancer and oral hygiene but successfully utilized internal, external, community, digital and social media marketing strategies and solidified my career path in the marketing industry."

Born in India, Sampat grew up in St. Thomas, US Virgin Islands, and now resides in the state of Washington with her husband. In 2020 Sampat used her social media skills to make her book, *Why Your Marketing Is Killing Your Business and What to Do About It*, an international Amazon bestseller. We met when she asked for editing help with the book.

Since the book was published her agency has grown 50 percent. She attributes many clients coming as a direct result of reading the book.

EVEN IF YOU ARE A CELEBRITY, THE PUBLISHER EXPECTS THE AUTHOR TO DO MOST OF THE PROMOTION

The dirty little secret of books is that unless you are a celebrity, the publisher expects the author to promote the book. Even if you are a celebrity, the publisher expects the author to do most of the promotion. Sampat feels the best place to promote a book is to go direct to readers through social media.

Sampat shared how her book marketing campaign was so successful. Here are Sampat's top ten ways to use social media to create a bestseller:

Start marketing with an intention. "Even if you are trying to simply do brand awareness about the book," says Sampat.

Learn how the social media algorithms such as Facebook and Instagram work and plan your strategy around it. The more you know, the better your marketing plan will be. "Whatever platform you are most active on, learn the algorithm for that platform," she says.

Leverage the organic reach by building an audience that would be genuinely interested in your book and topic. Sampat focused on people in business who are readers and liked content about books.

Make your marketing message about them, and not you, by highlighting the readers and spotlighting them in your marketing. "It's about them, it's not about you, is the attitude to have," says Sampat.

Share, share, share. Share content that is attached to the book but can be easily downloaded such as worksheets, graphs, and checklists.

Continuously show appreciation for the readers and the book. When you focus on connecting and not promotion, you will continue to do better with your marketing. Sampat always highlighted readers on Facebook and Instagram. She created a dialogue with readers and shared news about their business. "Nobody expected that from a random book they bought," said Sampat.

> WHEN YOU FOCUS ON CONNECTING AND NOT PROMOTION, YOU WILL CONTINUE TO DO BETTER WITH YOUR MARKETING

More share, share, share. On a weekly basis, share digestible content from the book such as quotes, lines, and chapter page photos.

Share your journey as an author. Readers want to connect with you. Give them a glimpse "behind the scenes."

Show off social proof. For example, share testimonials and reviews. Sampat would take screenshots from Amazon reviews to show what people had said.

Always offer book copies at webinars, conferences, and seminars. If you are teaching a course, use the book as required reading. And why not? Shouldn't students get your best thoughts?

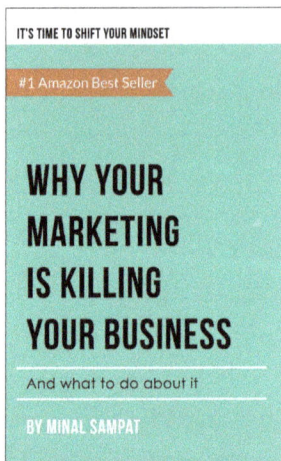

IT'S TIME TO SHIFT YOUR MINDSET

#1 Amazon Best Seller

WHY YOUR MARKETING IS KILLING YOUR BUSINESS

And what to do about it

BY MINAL SAMPAT

Cover design by Minal Sampat LLC

Steps To Shine A Spotlight On Your Book

When agency owners promote their books, they are really promoting their agency. Create the book with the end in mind. Here are twenty-five possible to-do items:

1. Testimonial blurbs for book back cover from famous people or companies the prospects in your niche would admire

2. Foreword for book written by a well-known person that prospects in your niche would admire

3. Website with PDF of table of contents and chapter one of book

4. Blog site where you post weekly blogs from book (this can be your personal LinkedIn page)

5. Twitter linked to blog site

6. Facebook linked to blog site

7. LinkedIn summaries of blog excerpts

8. E-zine (electronic tips newsletter) with articles from book

9. PR Newswire news releases on tips from book

10. Review copies sent to journalists and bloggers

11. Free speaking engagements (pro bono)

12. Fee speaking engagements (paid)

13. Small-scale seminars that author hosts

14. Webinars that author hosts or appears on

15. Conference based on the book

16. Book launch party

17. Flyer for book

18. Postcard for book

19. Business card for book

20. Articles excerpted from book chapters for publications

21. Internet publication column based on book

22. Print publication column based on book

23. Sponsorships for personalized copies of books

24. Institutional buyers that will buy books in quantity

25. Bulk book buyers that will buy books in quantity

Please know this: the magic is in the mix. Use the book to shine a spotlight on your work. Start by asking clients about their pains. Gather information on how to solve those worries, frustrations, and concerns.

Be the expert who educates people through books, speeches, and publicity on how they compare to their peers and the best ways to overcome their obstacles. The more prospects you inform how to solve their problems in general, the more they will hire you for the specifics. In the words of motivational speaker Zig Ziglar: "You can get whatever you want in life if you just help enough people get what they want."

How To Turn Bylined Trade Journal Articles Into Clients

Turn excerpts from your book into articles to help your agency find new clients.

A byline is a printed line of text that identifies the author of an article. The master of helping people get bylined trade articles placed is Russell Trahan, owner and president of PR/PR Public Relations. Amazingly, 100 percent of his clients get article placements.

He generously tells you how in his 2017 book, *Sell Yourself without Saying a Word: The Experts' Guide to Placing Articles in Print and Online.*

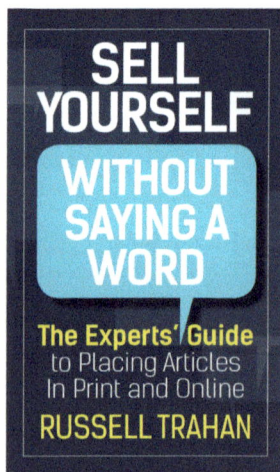

Cover design by Joni McPherson

Trahan credits the book with helping his twenty-year-old agency grow revenues by 25 percent.

"Having articles in association and trade publications makes you an authority in your field," says Trahan. "Your articles will help you gain name recognition on a national level."

Here is Trahan's step-by-step formula for a great article that magazines want to publish:

1. Create a provocative title.

2. Start off with a great opening sentence, also known as "the lede."

3. Open with a story.

4. Use the second paragraph to relate the dilemma to the readers.

5. Give three to eight tips, strategies, or steps the reader can take to solve the problem. Use bullet points or numbers.

6. Give a very brief, one-paragraph summary with a call to action at the end.

7. Keep the word count around eight hundred to one thousand words.

8. Include a resource box at the end of the article with your contact information.

9. In the resource box, mention your book, company, product, or service. Also mention any CDs, DVDs, or online videos you have.

10. And some don'ts: don't promote yourself or your book within the article, don't write it in first person, and

don't give your opinion but state facts instead. You promote the book in the resource box at the end.

For many would-be bylined authors, the obstacle is the provocative title. Publicity expert Joan Stewart, creator of the www.publicityhound.com website, uses a fill-in-the-blank approach for brainstorming article ideas. Consider some of her suggestions:

- A Quiz: Test Your _____ Smarts
- Common Errors that Kill _____
- The Great _____ Dilemma
- Mastering the Art of _____
- Top 10 _____ Dos and Don'ts
- 5 No-Fail Strategies for _____
- 25 Quick _____ Tips to Use Now

Next, how do you turn the article into high-paying clients? Here are five ideas from Trahan on how to leverage your media placements:

Make your resource box at the end of the article memorable. Be sure to mention credentials and contact information.

Buy reprints and send copies to past clients, current prospects, and advocates.

Put a media page on your website. List all the articles that are published.

Make a list. Put a concise list of your magazine publication history into your bio.

Leverage articles into speeches. Use your printed articles to market to associations of that industry as a speaker.

As Trahan says: "Media credentials speak loudly on your behalf. Whether you've been speaking or writing for a few months or many years, being quoted in the media makes you an instant expert."

Marketing With A Bookism

THE REAL JOB OF AN AGENCY AUTHOR IS TO SHINE A SPOTLIGHT ON THEIR BOOK. TO QUOTE AGENCY GREAT DAVID OGILVY, "YOU CAN'T SAVE SOULS IN AN EMPTY CHURCH."

*"How about one of those sunny old grandpas
who make things look honest?"*

12

Think Magnificent Seven

If you know me, you know I am a movie buff.

A favorite film is *The Magnificent Seven*, a 1960 American western film directed by John Sturges and starring Yul Brynner, Eli Wallach, Steve McQueen, and Horst Buchholz. The motion picture is an Old West–style remake of Akira Kurosawa's 1954 Japanese-language film *Seven Samurai*. Some prefer the 2016 remake starring Denzel Washington and Chris Pratt.

In my training events for agency owners, I often talk about "The Magnificent Seven" ways to attract high-paying clients. Here is a list in rank order:

1. Free or low-cost small-scale seminars.
The best proactive tactic you can employ is to regularly invite prospects by mail and email to small seminars or group consultations. If your prospects are spread out geographically, you can do these briefings via webinars and Zoominars. These can't be sixty-minute commercials. You need to present valuable information about how to solve the problems that your prospects are facing, and then a little mention of your services.

2. How-to speeches at client industry meetings. People want to hire experts, and an expert is invited to speak. Actively seek out forums to speak and list past and future speaking dates on your website.

3. How-to articles in a client-oriented press. Better than any brochure is the how-to article that appears in a publication that your target clients read.

4. Community and association involvement. Everyone likes to do business with people they know, like, and trust. You need to get involved and "circulate to percolate," as one Ohio State University professor of a colleague used to say.

5. Networking and trade shows. This is an excellent way to gather business cards and ask for permission to include them on your e-newsletter list.

6. Internet game plan. For agency authors, this is the one-two punch of LinkedIn and YouTube. Use your LinkedIn profile like a blog site. Make sure it has fresh content every thirty days. Create a series of under-two-minute how-to videos based on the book content for your YouTube channel.

7. Paid ballroom workshops. This is the strategy of renting out the ballroom at the local Marriott or Hilton and charging for an all-day or half-day workshop. Participants should take away a substantial packet of useful information from your firm (and a delicious meal too).

More About Those Zoominars

Not to be an alarmist, but many prospects are testing positive for Zoom fatigue.

Well, get over it. Zoom is your new best friend when it comes to business development.

Time and distance are keeping you and your prospects apart. If you serve clients that are located throughout the country or even in different countries, the silver lining to the pandemic is the widespread adoption of Zoom.

This has given rise to the Zoominar, a virtual seminar that allows you to host inexpensive meetings for people from anywhere.

While generating high-paying clients through small-scale seminars is a proven marketing strategy for agency owners, times have been tough. Many agency owners are frustrated that they can't gather prospects into a room like they used to. Others are frustrated by a lack of turnout for the Zoominars they do host.

Here are steps to increase attendance for your next lead generation event on Zoom:

WHILE GENERATING HIGH-PAYING CLIENTS THROUGH SMALL-SCALE SEMINARS IS A PROVEN MARKETING STRATEGY FOR AGENCY OWNERS, TIMES HAVE BEEN TOUGH

1. Choose clarity over cleverness when writing your Zoominar invites.

2. Develop a checklist and timeline of your pre- and post-Zoominar activities.

3. Determine your target audience of prospects. LinkedIn is a great tool to find people if you know details about them (we entered all that info about ourselves in LinkedIn and it is searchable).

4. Use informal research to pretest the topics to make sure the one you choose has the most appeal to your target audience. A great option is always: "The Three Biggest Blunders _____ _____ Make When Doing _____ _____."

5. Make sure emails, social media postings, web landing pages, and LinkedIn messages convey a first-class image for you.

6. Confirm registrations forty-eight hours before the event by email. If you want to be a business development ninja, reach out and call prospects to tell them you are looking forward to meeting them and ask if they have any specific questions or areas they want you to cover.

IF YOU WANT TO BE A BUSINESS DEVELOPMENT NINJA, REACH OUT AND CALL PROSPECTS TO TELL THEM YOU ARE LOOKING FORWARD TO MEETING THEM AND ASK IF THEY HAVE ANY SPECIFIC QUESTIONS OR AREAS THEY WANT YOU TO COVER

7. Deliver seminar content that is of real value. Make it a no-selling zone. Delivering a thinly disguised sales pitch is the kiss of death.

8. Make it easy for the prospect to have a strategy call later. Offer this briefly during the seminar and send the follow-up offer by email. Make it clear it is a no-selling call and honor that.

9. For the strategy call the recommended agenda is to get clarity around their goals, assets, and roadblocks and to learn from you how others have gotten from where they are to where they want to go.

10. Conduct organized follow-ups to stay in touch with the people who signed up to attend but did not make it. These are the forgotten few. They are interested in the topic, but something came up, and the easiest item on the day to say no to is the Zoominar. About 50 percent who sign up do not show up, and they are still great prospects.

CONDUCT ORGANIZED FOLLOW-UPS TO STAY IN TOUCH WITH THE PEOPLE WHO SIGNED UP TO ATTEND BUT DID NOT MAKE IT

11. Measure, measure, measure. Be sure to measure all aspects of the program to see what could be improved. Measure how many were invited, how many accepted, how many attended, how many who attended booked a strategy call, how

many kept the call, and how many of those callers became clients.

Because the number one challenge for agency owners is creating new clients, Zoominars are a dignified way to network with prospects and develop new referral sources.

One more thought about being clear rather than clever. As management visionary Peter Drucker once said, you must answer certain questions: What is our business? Who is our client? What does our client consider valuable? The secret to Zoominar business development success lies in the answers to those three questions.

Ways To Get Clients To See What You're Saying

These are emotional times and to attract high-paying clients you need to be a better storyteller. That means telling stories that prospects can see in their mind's eye.

Using innovative visual thinking techniques can help you to increase understanding of, and gain buy-in for, your ideas.

That's the advice of Todd Cherches, a TEDx speaker ("The Power of Visual Thinking") and the author of the 2020 book *VisuaLeadership: Leveraging the Power of Visual Thinking in Leadership and in Life*.

"We all know that a picture is worth a thousand words, but do you know *why* that is?" asks Cherches. "How can you leverage that concept to grow your business?"

Cherches says that when we use visuals—and visual language—it enhances our ability to get people to focus on what we're saying, increases understanding, and gets people to remember. What he simply refers to as: "attention, comprehension, and retention."

So, how can we do this? Cherches identifies four key ways:

Visual imagery is about using pictures, illustrations, drawings, and even descriptive visual language that paints a picture with words.

Mental models could include maps, graphs, charts, diagrams, or any other framework that enables others to envision your idea.

WHEN WE USE VISUALS— AND VISUAL LANGUAGE— IT ENHANCES OUR ABILITY TO GET PEOPLE TO FOCUS ON WHAT WE'RE SAYING, INCREASES UNDERSTANDING, AND GETS PEOPLE TO REMEMBER

Metaphors or analogies compare like things to help you explain what you're talking about in a creative and visual way.

Visual storytelling—from cautionary tales to success stories—uses narrative to help bring your ideas to life in an engaging, human, memorable, and visual way.

"So, keep in mind that while a picture is worth a thousand words, the right words and pictures just might end up being worth a million, or more, dollars," says Cherches.

Marketing With A Bookism

RESEARCH IS ALL WELL AND GOOD, BUT YOUR BOOK SHOULD BE MORE THAN AN ECHO CHAMBER.

13

Speaking Of Books

There's plenty of advice out there on public speaking tips, but for many agency owners, overcoming the challenge of public speaking first involves managing the stress that comes with it. Elevated levels of stress can affect your brain's memory and spatial awareness capacities, which can make a simple speech feel like an endurance race.

Jamie Sussel Turner, an award-winning author of two books on stress, and a TEDx Speaker Coach, was an expert on helping people overcome their fear. According to the late Turner, "If public speaking makes you want to puke," you'll need to dig deep and shift how you perceive both yourself and your audience. We met when I helped her edit a book on helping business owners to have less stress.

"What we believe influences how we behave," Turner explained. "When you rewire your beliefs, you'll turn your stress on its head. Adopting new beliefs will lead to new thinking, which will lead to new confidence."

Turner said there are five stress-inducing beliefs every public speaker needs to process and shut down. Whether you're aiming for a TED talk stage or preparing for a Zoom meeting with a single prospective client, shift your mind about these five beliefs:

WHETHER YOU'RE AIMING FOR A TED TALK STAGE OR PREPARING FOR A ZOOM MEETING WITH A SINGLE PROSPECTIVE CLIENT, SHIFT YOUR MIND ABOUT THESE FIVE BELIEFS

It's all about me. "Believing your talk is all about you leaves out a crucial element—your audience. When I'm on stage I imagine the spotlight shining on the audience, reminding me I'm here to serve the people who have taken their time to come and hear me speak."

My future is riding on this speech. "You may feel like this one speech is crucial for attracting clients or growing your business. Remind yourself that it's just one talk. You will have other opportunities. Focus instead on what you can learn from this speech and discover how to rock your next talk even more."

I must nail my talk. "This belief goes to the heart of perfectionism, especially if you expect your every point needs to be delivered just as you have planned. This is a formula for feeling shaky and uncertain on the stage. Instead, shift your focus to being present with your audience. They have no idea what you've planned to say. Often what I say in place of what I've planned is even more powerful."

The audience is judging me. "Yes, they are. And guess what? There's nothing you can do about it. If you try to be anything but yourself to please the audience, they will spot your lack of authenticity in a nanosecond. So, accept that being judged is out of your control—and let it go."

I am not enough of an expert. "This belief speaks to imposter syndrome, the feeling that you are not worthy, and may be unveiled as a fraud. Instead recognize your worth as being uniquely yours. No one else has your experience or ideas. Yes, there may be experts who know more than you. But their delivery or stories don't resonate with the audience like yours. Someone in a position of authority thinks you're a worthy speaker on your topic, right? You'll feel more confidence and less stress when you arrive on the stage believing in your expertise."

So how do you unlearn thoughts and fears that might be subconscious or deeply embedded? No big secret there; it takes practice.

"Challenge your beliefs before you meet your next audience. Write them down and speak them aloud," Turner advised. "It might sound like this: I'm here to serve my audience. This is just one speech among many. I'll be more confident when I'm not trying to be perfect. I can't control their judgments. I am enough of an expert."

I'M HERE TO SERVE MY AUDIENCE, THIS IS JUST ONE SPEECH AMONG MANY

Marketing With A Bookism

IF YOU ARE SPEAKING WITHOUT A BOOK, YOU ARE JUST PREACHING AND NOT TEACHING. WHEN I AM BOOKED TO SPEAK I ASK THE ORGANIZER, "DOES IT MAKE SENSE FOR ME TO GET EVERYONE EXCITED ABOUT THE TOPIC AND THEN SKIP TOWN WITHOUT GIVING THEM THE INSTRUCTION BOOK?"

14

Podcasting: That's Infotainment

Networking has always been a top way to attract high-paying clients, but podcasting is a new spin on the strategy.

Five years ago, Jodi Katz started her top-rated podcast, *Where Brains Meet Beauty*, to network within her industry in a way that felt rightsized for her personality.

"I've always been someone who feels really at ease one-on-one with new people, but I freeze when in a group," says Katz. "The bite-sized interview format of my show felt both safe and empowering to me as I explored a medium that was new to me."

Katz has been a respected voice in the beauty and wellness industry for almost twenty years, fifteen of them as founder and creative director of Base Beauty Creative Agency. She started her career in advertising at the legendary agency BBDO, followed by positions on the editorial side of *Cosmopolitan* and *Glamour* magazines.

"I saw the podcast as a way to dig deeper and learn more about my peers than I could by quickly asking about their kids or their last job while rushing into a meeting or during chitchat at industry cocktail parties," says Katz. "The target is the intersection of professional desires and personal backstories. I don't need to hear about product launches or upcoming marketing campaigns in this forum—there are plenty of other ways I stay current on all of that. I want to learn about my guests' childhood dreams, their motivations, and goals and how they feel about their journey so far."

To ensure that the wisdom of her guests reaches a wider audience, Katz asked me for editing help in writing a book based on the podcast titled *Facing the Seduction of Success*, which was published in 2022. I asked Katz to share some tips for getting more success out of a podcast:

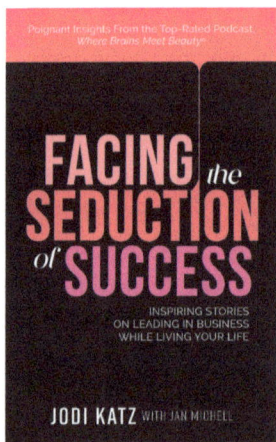

Cover design by Elisa Vitale

Listen to other shows in your genre. "My show is rooted in the beauty industry, and there are many podcasts devoted to beauty products, tips, and tricks," says Katz. "For my show to stand out, I needed a differentiating angle."

Don't be rigid. "The beauty of this medium is that you can set your own guardrails," says Katz. "In the early episodes, I recorded shows remotely, which made it easier for me to schedule guests. Then we moved to face-to-face interviews, which made for much richer content and a more fun listening experience for our fans. But once Covid started, we were back to recording remotely. To celebrate our fifth anniversary, we innovated the remote format with live streaming—each episode is now recorded via YouTube Live, so our fans can watch the show get made in real-time. For our classic podcast listeners, the episodes are still available for download in their favorite podcast apps."

FOR MY SHOW TO STAND OUT, I NEEDED A DIFFERENTIATING ANGLE

Think long-term. "No matter your goal for a podcast, no success is reached overnight," adds Katz. "Think of this as an ongoing part of your workload, something that over a long time has the possibility to create real impact. But five or ten episodes won't get you there. Keep going, one step at a time, and momentum will come."

Recycle your podcast in many ways. "Be efficient with your time and resources by taking full advantage of your rich podcast content," says Katz. "Post transcripts of your shows on your website to feed Google rich SEO, use pull quotes from the show to reach new listeners via social media, and make partnerships with like-minded industry events to promote their efforts while giving visibility to your show. Be creative here to work smarter, not harder."

Over two hundred episodes later, the show's role in her life goes way beyond networking.

"It's both free therapy and free business coaching for me, guided by the talented and ambitious guests that are generous with their time and vulnerability," says Katz.

Podcasting Is Not For Everyone

If you are going to podcast, be original or don't bother. That is the advice of Dusty Weis, whose podcast *Lead Balloon* was selected by *Adweek* as the 2020 "Marketing Podcast of the Year."

Creating another boring, ho-hum podcast is a dusty road to failure.

"We have a failure problem in the fields of PR and marketing," says Weis. "Not the act of failure, but the fear of it. Failure has become so stigmatized that many operations would rather embrace formulaic mediocrity than risk trying something new because of the fear that it might fail."

Should you not do a podcast because it might fail? Perhaps. In a podcast world with more than two million shows (and climbing), Weis says you're not going to make waves doing what's already been done a thousand times before.

Be original. Be bold. Be interesting. As the late advertising great David Ogilvy said, you can't bore people into buying. Podcasting might not be expensive to do, but the opportunity cost of your time and energy is huge if you are podcasting to attract high-paying clients.

"When I launched the *Lead Balloon* podcast, I was putting my content-marketing-money-where-my-mouth-is on that imperative," says Weis. "My customers are PR and marketing practitioners, so I needed to make a show that appealed to them."

As he started to research the other shows in the PR and marketing genre, he was dumbfounded by the formulaic nature of so many of them. *But why?* he wondered, since this a creative field and it's full of creative people.

"So, I turned hard into the imperative, 'Be Original, or Don't Bother,'" says Weis. "Where other marketing podcasters focus on quantity of content, I focus on quality. Where others do thought leadership, I do storytelling. Where others focus on accelerating their cadence, I spend forty to fifty hours getting an episode just right."

And *Lead Balloon* celebrates learning through failure.

Marketing With A Bookism

WHEN SOMEONE ASKS YOU A GREAT QUESTION LIKE, "WOULD YOU LIKE TO BE ON MY PODCAST?" YOU SHOULD PAUSE THREE SECONDS FOR DIGNITY AND THEN REPLY, "THANK YOU FOR ASKING. YES, I WOULD."

©Glasbergen
glasbergen.com

GLASBERGEN

"Your agency has a critical morale problem.
My advice is to go from desk to desk licking people's faces."

15

Why You Should Maybe Coauthor A Book

Ken Blanchard, a man who has sold millions and millions of business books, once told me in an interview: "You know, I have never authored a business book."

"Ken, are you pulling my leg?" I asked. "You've authored more than fifty business books."

"No, I have *coauthored* fifty business books," said Blanchard. "I know what I know, I want to know what other people know too."

Blanchard's impact as a thought leader is far reaching. *The One Minute Manager*—the iconic 1982 classic that he coauthored with the late Spencer Johnson—sold more than thirteen million copies and in 2015 was revised and released as *The New One Minute Manager*.

Blanchard has now coauthored sixty-five books whose combined sales total more than twenty-eight million copies. His groundbreaking works—including *Raving Fans*, *The Secret*, and *Leading at a Higher Level*, to name just a few—have been translated into forty-seven languages. In 2005 Blanchard was inducted into Amazon's Hall of Fame as one of the top twenty-five best-selling authors of all time.

In January 2021, the world lost a great author, Diane Gage Lofgren. Or should I say a great coauthor. She taught me how to be a coauthor back in the early 1990s. Lofgren taught others to be a great coauthor, too.

Here are some important lessons Lofgren taught me about being a coauthor:

Decide who will be listed as the lead author. The author who has the most claim on the content of the book is the lead author. Gage was the second author on my book. I was the second author on a book I coauthored with Tom Searcy, because the idea was his. Blanchard is often the second author listed on many of his books. It is not determined by who is most famous or has the biggest platform.

Decide if the book ownership percentage will be split 50/50 or 51/49. Some of my books are 50/50 and some are 51/49. One best-selling author I know will only do 51/49 deals because he was burned on a 50/50 deal after he had a falling out with his coauthor. She then blocked him from using the book topic as a speech topic. If you own 51 percent, you are in the driver's seat when it comes to future decisions such as a revised edition or selling the book to a traditional publisher if you indie published.

Decide what the split of royalties will be. This can be 50/50 or some other split. I have even heard of a 95/5 deal. Everything in life is a negotiation.

Decide how you will approach the writing. One way is to split the chapters and have each writer do half the chapters and then trade for editing. Another strategy is to have one author write the first drafts and the other author write the polished chapters. There are many right answers, but the approach must be decided upon in advance and agreed upon as equitable. I have coauthored ten books and each approach was different.

Decide how you will approach the editing and proofing. Any book worth writing is worth writing a first draft that is sucky. The real magic happens in the editing. Proofing is the last step, and the coauthors are not best suited to this because they are too close.

Decide how you will market the book. In my experience, the number one way to promote a book is to talk about it in speeches, podcasts, and radio and TV interviews. More people are impacted by hearing about the book than by reading the book.

Decide how you will split paid speaking engagements because of the book. An expert with a best-selling business book speaks in the $5,000 to $10,000 range. Coauthors should decide how to split this when speaking invitations come in unexpectedly. The truth is coauthors must market themselves to gain speaking opportunities. I follow the "You Eat What You Hunt" philosophy: if you book the gig, you get all of the fee unless you invite your author to co-present.

The bottom line: Two minds are better than one when it comes to a great business book. Great business books share the why, the how, and the what's next for readers. The readers supply the when. Overall, the coauthors must create a book they love because if they don't love the book, how can they get others to love it?

Marketing With A Bookism

PUBLISHING THE BOOK IS THE STARTING LINE, NOT THE FINISH LINE.

"This is the only product claim that legal would allow."

16

Rainmaking Tools

What is the second biggest pain for agency owners? Not enough time for business development.

Technology is available today to assist businesses in every industry to bring all or part of their operations to the cloud. Now is the time to bring your marketing to the cloud.

"Global enterprises have been investing in automation for decades," says marketing expert Clare Price, author of the 2022 book *Smart Marketing Execution*. "That investment really showed its value during the pandemic years of 2020 and 2021. Because of automation employees were able to quickly transition to remote work during the early lockdowns."

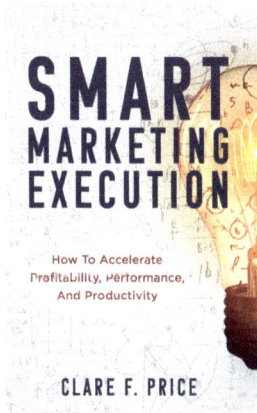

Cover design by SP Book Design

Price is CEO of Octain Growth Systems, a global strategic planning consulting firm that works with companies to improve profitability, productivity, and operating efficiency. She notes that large companies were better positioned for the hybrid work environment that includes both at-the-office and remote workers because they had the automated tools in place.

According to Price, small enterprises and solopreneurs weren't so lucky. They had to scramble to recover momentum when the lockdowns occurred. The result? "Small business owners now have more appreciation for the power of automation to drive operating efficiencies in their organizations," says Price.

BUSINESS OWNERS NOW HAVE MORE APPRECIATION FOR THE POWER OF AUTOMATION TO DRIVE OPERATING EFFICIENCIES IN THEIR ORGANIZATIONS

Technology is available today to assist business owners and marketers in every industry to bring all or part of their operations to the cloud. Price recommends you automate the following five marketing functions:

Appointment Booking. "Bringing your appointment scheduling online frees you from the mundane. It gives customers flexibility and protects your time when you need it," advises Price. "These are worth a look. Calendaring software like Calendly and CalendarWiz are great options for booking individual client appointments. For a more robust appointment-setting solution, and virtual administrative support for class scheduling and training, try TimeTap. TimeTap includes features for multiple locations, class scheduling, customized booking forms, and automatic payments.

SimplyBook.me is an online booking system for professional services companies that offers online booking, notifications, payments, and marketing incentives like coupons, gift cards, memberships, and product sales. In addition, SimplyBook.me offers listing in their professional services directory."

Proposal Software. "If your company submits proposals for jobs manually, especially in professional services, I strongly recommend investing in proposal software. Not only does proposal software drastically cut the nonbillable time you spend developing your proposal, but it also monitors the prospects, response by tracking when, what, and how they view what you sent them. Imagine knowing when your prospect read your proposal instead of wondering and sending blind follow-ups. Now imagine knowing what pages caught their attention. Was it benefits? Features? Pricing? Knowing this better equips you to send a follow-up designed to appropriately respond to their specific interests. That's exactly what proposal software like PandaDoc, Proposify, and BidSketch can do for you. Most offer a limited free version or trial," says Price.

Email Marketing Systems. "If your primary marketing efforts are built around email marketing, you can find many effective and inexpensive solutions on the market today," states Price. "Marketing automation software automates many baseline marketing functions that enable your team to excel at demand and lead generation. Options run from email marketing systems to sophisticated demand and lead generation and prospecting platforms. Marketing automation is a critical success component of digital and social media marketing. My top six choices for marketing automation are ActiveCampaign, Autopilot, Keap (formerly Infusionsoft), HubSpot, SharpSpring, and Ontraport."

Customer Relationship Management (CRM). "A robust CRM tool is one cloud sales enablement tool no business should be without," states Price. "CRM software solutions are all about building customer relationships. They enable your sales team to connect with prospects and track their activity with your business from first connect to close of sale. CRM systems include contact management, lead management, opportunity management, and sales forecasting. Some integrate with marketing automation systems—theirs and others. My top five picks for CRM are Salesforce Sales Cloud, Nutshell, Copper, Pipedrive, and Zoho CRM."

Customer Service. "To make remote work, you need to keep clients happy by delivering a seamless customer experience (CX) to every client. They expect support through a range of channels and devices as quickly as possible. Clients now demand an Amazon-like experience from every supplier. Phone and email support alone just don't cut it anymore, given today's challenging times," states Price. "Any small business owner can radically change their customer service experience with online CX investments...a technology to invest in for customer service is live chat. Live chat changes your website from a static information site to a live customer resource center. It allows you to reduce response times from hours to seconds. Most importantly, it helps you increase sales. The American Marketing Association found that B2B companies who used live chat saw, on average, a 20 percent increase in conversions. The three live chat software solutions I'd recommend checking out are: LiveChat, Zendesk, and Olark."

Bottom line: Put simply, automation has top-line and bottom-line benefits that drive profits, productivity, and efficiencies for your team, no matter how small.

Marketing With A Bookism

STORIES IN BUSINESS BOOKS DO NOT HAVE TO BE 100 PERCENT FACTUAL; NAMES AND DETAILS CAN BE CHANGED TO MAINTAIN CONFIDENTIALITY. LITERARY LICENSE IS NOT A SIN.

17

Attitude Of Gratitude

Smart agency owners leverage their books with gratitude for more referrals. They appreciate the four magic words in the English language: "I know a guy."

Referrals make a difference. You want to be the person they refer others to.

"If you deal with CEOs and other C-suite people, a sophisticated and nuanced referral approach is absolutely necessary," says Scott Hamilton, founder of the Executive Next Practices Institute, a network of enterprise-level key executives where I am regularly invited to speak. "With the C-suite, budget and RFPs are never an issue. It is a relationship-based sale that is fast forwarded via the well-crafted referral."

Much of this strategy I owe a debt of gratitude to my partner at Indie Books International, business coach extraordinaire Mark LeBlanc, my coauthor on several books. Here are solid referral actions:

Whip your CRM into shape first. Digitize your outreach with a CRM like Nimble. This is a simple, smart CRM for Office 365 and G Suite teams. You can automatically combine contacts, social media connections, in-boxes, and calendar appointments. Some of its clients include GoDaddy, Coldwell Banker, and Upwork. This app allows you to tag a contact multiple times so you can easily make lists. However, do not just tag a referral as a referral. Are they an advocate or an affiliate?

Build a list of twenty-five advocates. Advocates, also known as cheerleaders, are champions of you and your business who give you referrals for no monetary consideration. Advocates believe in you. An advocate likes to tell prospects that they do not receive any compensation for referring you; they just want the prospect to be well cared for. To make the advocate list there must be evidence of referring business to you. Why only twenty-five? You should contact them on a regular basis, and more than twenty-five can become unwieldy. There is nothing wrong with giving small gifts to advocates to show your appreciation, but it cannot be a quid pro quo for every referral or every referral that becomes a client.

Build a list of twenty-five affiliates. Affiliates, also known as partners, are people who will recommend you but expect a financial reward. To make the list they must agree to be willing to refer you for a fee. Typically, this might be in the form of a percentage, with 10 percent being a typical fee, but this will vary by industry. Some professionals, like attorneys, cannot pay referral fees. You should memorialize the agreement in writing, such as an email. This is not legal advice (I am not an attorney and do not give legal advice); this is practical because you should not rely on your memory.

> THERE IS NOTHING WRONG WITH GIVING SMALL GIFTS TO ADVOCATES TO SHOW YOUR APPRECIATION, BUT IT CANNOT BE A QUID PRO QUO FOR EVERY REFERRAL OR EVERY REFERRAL THAT BECOMES A CLIENT

Decide who you will be an advocate or an affiliate for. As you network, identify people who might make great referral sources. Start with this opener: "If you would be open to a conversation about being referral partners, it would be greatly appreciated." "If" and "conversation" are soft knocks at the door.

Contact advocates and affiliates monthly. It is not the job of the advocates and affiliates to remember you; it is your job to remind them that you exist. Use a variety of means; do not just rely on email. Utilize other channels like texting, LinkedIn messages, Facebook Messenger, and the telephone. Be brief because you want to be aware of their time.

Teach your advocates and affiliates your elevator pitch. "Elevator pitches addressing a prospect's threat get you in earlier in the process and at a higher level," says Bryan Gray, agency owner of Revenue Path Group and author of the book *The Priority Sale*. "Today elevator pitches can award you the next fifteen minutes of attention at the right level in an organization."

Give if you want to get. If you want to receive referrals, you need to give referrals. Let the law of reciprocation work in your favor. A place to start is to reach out and give concrete recommendations on LinkedIn. Be honest and specific. You will be amazed at how many people want to return the favor.

Snail mail them little gifts to remind them you appreciate them. I have sent packets of seeds, baseball cards to wish them a happy spring, unusual paper clips, multi-colored Post-it notes, and other items I find at a dollar store. Include a note expressing your gratitude. Many referral sources say they look forward to the lumpy envelopes I send.

Be ready with an email response. Chance favors the prepared. When someone sends a referral by email, I am ready with a preset response loaded into my signature files in Microsoft Outlook. I send the email to the referrer and the prospect. I thank the referrer for the introduction, and I formally introduce myself in seven sentences and then provide a link to my calendar for a no-cost strategy call.

Offer up a template for an email they can send out about you. In mine I mention the relationship and why they might want to get in touch with me. I make it easy for my advocates and affiliates to pass along my information.

Close the loop. Do your utmost to close the loop with the referrer to tell them what happened and that you appreciate the referral.

Here is the bottom line: The time has come to rededicate to solid business development strategies such as accelerating referrals.

Marketing With A Bookism

EVERY GREAT AGENCY STORY HAS THREE CHARACTERS: A CLIENT WITH A PROBLEM, A MESS-CREATING NEMESIS, AND AN AGENCY MENTOR WHO PROVIDES WISDOM SO THE CLIENT CAN GO FROM MESS TO SUCCESS.

18

Creating A Great Book Is A Team Sport

Writing is a team sport. Don't go it alone.

You could try the loner approach by renting a cabin in the mountains and not coming out until you have a manuscript. I call that the *Misery* approach (think Stephen King's book and movie).

Getting published is too important of a variable in the marketing success quotient to go it alone and be miserable. Don't let the excuse that you're not a good writer prevent you from publishing a book. A ghostwriter can take your rough notes, conversations, and ideas and turn them into something that's polished and well-written.

But there is a cost associated with that. Another option is a developmental editor. This type of editor is your teammate in the publishing process. They bring to the team experience, ideas, and writing skills.

A successful consultant recently told me: "When I hired you, I thought you would take my thoughts and just turn them into something wonderful. But you didn't do that. You worked

DON'T LET THE EXCUSE THAT YOU'RE NOT A GOOD WRITER PREVENT YOU FROM PUBLISHING A BOOK

with me to make them the best thoughts that could come from me. I see now that was the right thing to do. This book is my book, and it has been a lifelong dream to get it published."

What is essential and can never be farmed out: your ability to present quality information and your ideas. Your material should spark an "aha" in your readers and ignite them to reach greater heights. If you can prompt someone else to succeed, then you will have succeeded too.

Marketing With A Bookism

I DO NOT WANT TO TELL AGENCY OWNERS HOW TO LIVE THEIR LIVES, BUT IF YOU ARE NOT MARKETING WITH A BOOK YOU ARE MAKING A STUPENDOUS MISTAKE.

19

Cracking The Business Fiction Book Code

If you want to attract high-paying clients with a book, lose the rhetoric and engage in storytelling.

What do these client-attracting books have in common: *The One Minute Manager*, *Who Moved My Cheese*, and *The Five Dysfunctions of a Team*?

They are all examples of a business novella, which is a work of fiction.

Books open many doors to help attract clients, such as speaking engagements, podcast interviews, book reviews, blogs, articles, and workshops based on the book. The book is the key that creates opportunities for prospects to experience you.

Instead of writing a typical nonfiction business advice book based on your expertise, consider writing a piece of fiction.

Advances in neurosciences prove that prospects make decisions based on emotion, not logic. But how do you access the emotional part of the brain? The answer is to weave your message into a story. Human brains are hardwired for stories.

"We have always preferred books that were told as a tale, a fable, or a story, whether fiction or nonfiction," says Gary Maag, coauthor along with David Kalinowski of *New Direc-*

ADVANCES IN NEUROSCIENCES PROVE THAT PROSPECTS MAKE DECISIONS BASED ON EMOTION, NOT LOGIC. BUT HOW DO YOU ACCESS THE EMOTIONAL PART OF THE BRAIN?

tions: A Competitive Intelligence Tale and their 2022 book, The CI-Driven CEO. "When reading books from authors such as Ken Blanchard, Matthew Kelly, and Patrick Lencioni, who get their messages across in a more interesting way, it hit us that we should take that approach for a book in our industry of competitive intelligence."

Maag and Kalinowski are the leaders of Proactive Worldwide, a twenty-seven-year-old marketing consulting firm with clients on three continents. About 85 percent of the firm's clients are in the Fortune 500.

"Writing our book as a story was also a fun way to dispel the myths or beliefs held by some when they hear the words 'competitive intelligence' that somehow this equates with corporate espionage, spying, midnight rendezvous, secret handshakes, and decoder rings," said Kalinowski.

As they read the various books in their space, Maag and Kalinowski realized all were lacking an engaging way to get readers to understand what competitive intelligence is and how it adds value to any organization. So, in 2011 they decided to educate business professionals through the power of storytelling. We met when they asked for help editing their upcoming business novella.

"One of the biggest reasons we wrote the book as a tale was that we wanted to provide C-suite executives something they would find different and interesting enough to spend their time reading and do so fairly quickly," said Maag. "We wanted it to be an effortless and light-hearted read that they enjoyed and could easily digest in a three-hour plane ride, tarmac to tarmac, on their next business trip."

These authors figured telling a story that they found highly entertaining and informative would be a winning combination and be more effective to an audience than common rhetoric.

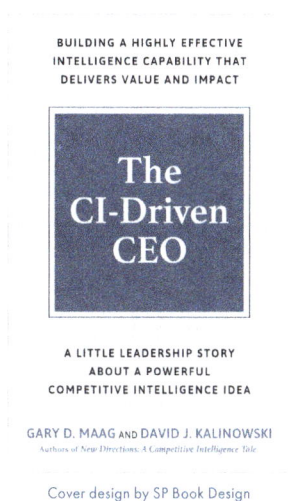

BUILDING A HIGHLY EFFECTIVE
INTELLIGENCE CAPABILITY THAT
DELIVERS VALUE AND IMPACT

The CI-Driven CEO

A LITTLE LEADERSHIP STORY
ABOUT A POWERFUL
COMPETITIVE INTELLIGENCE IDEA

GARY D. MAAG and DAVID J. KALINOWSKI
Authors of *New Directions: A Competitive Intelligence Tale*

Cover design by SP Book Design

Here are my three best tips for creating a compelling business novella:

Tip #1: Make sure your book solves a problem. Before you write word one you must be clear on what business problem you are solving. People have three basic problems: a lack of money, a lack of health, and a lack of love. Start there but get specific.

Tip #2: Keep your book light, tight, and bright. You are not writing the great American novel. Some of the biggest business novella bestsellers of all time are short: *The Greatest*

Salesman in the World, by Og Mandino, comes in at 130 pages; Spencer Johnson's training and development master-piece—*Who Moved My Cheese?*—is only ninety-five pages; and *The Go-Giver: A Little Story about a Powerful Business Idea* by Bob Burg and John David Mann is 132 pages.

Tip #3: Create nine characters. Each character has a role in telling the story. For illustration purposes, consider the characters from the original *Star Wars* film (for full disclosure, I own a tiny amount of Disney stock, which owns the *Star Wars* franchise). These characters I have learned from my various screenwriting mentors:

> **Hero.** This is the main character of the story, also known as the protagonist. We see the story through the eyes and ears of the main character. In *Star Wars*, this is Luke Skywalker.
>
> **Sidekick.** A hero needs a sidekick to share his or her thoughts with. Have the hero tell the sidekick what he or she is thinking. In *Star Wars*, these are the droids.
>
> **Nemesis.** Someone needs to oppose the hero for conflict. This person does not need to be a villain or evil. They are the antagonist. In *Star Wars*, it's the emperor (but he is extremely evil).
>
> **Mentor.** The hero can't succeed alone. Enter the mentor. In *Star Wars*, this is Yoda. This character is the voice of wisdom and experience (hint: it is really you in disguise).
>
> **Confounder.** This character is not the nemesis or antagonist. This person may or may not work in

concert with the nemesis. It just might be a character that gets in the way of the hero to create conflict. Without conflict, the story is too boring to read. In *Star Wars*, this is Darth Vader (plot spoiler, he is Luke's father).

Logic. The hero needs teammates on the journey. One character is the voice of reason. In *Star Wars*, this is Princess Leia Organa.

Heart. The hero needs teammates on the journey. One character is the voice of emotion. In *Star Wars*, this is Chewbacca. Chewie wails pure emotion.

Skeptic. The hero needs teammates on the journey. One character is the voice of skepticism. In *Star Wars*, this is Han "I got a bad feeling about this" Solo.

Recruit. The recruit is a trainee. The recruit's role in the story is for exposition. Recruits are stand-ins for the audience as other characters explain to them the world they are in. (In *Star Wars*, Luke Skywalker and others fulfill this role.)

Maag and Kalinowski use many characters to propel their story.

"While competitive intelligence is certainly an exciting discipline in every industry to piece together and analyze fragments of knowledge, it isn't quite as sexy as spy craft," says Kalinowski. "We want people to think more of investigative reporters like Murphy Brown or Clark Kent and less of secret agents like James Bond when it comes to competitive intelligence."

In *The CI-Driven CEO*, Jack, the imperfect chief competitive officer of Hewitt Games, faces a huge challenge when an unexpected competitor enters the scene and threatens the lifeblood of his company. When he is appointed the interim CEO, he must find a way to create a deeply embedded, CI-friendly culture and develop a strategy to outmaneuver the competition before all is lost.

As they examined various books in their space, Maag and Kalinowski realized all were lacking an engaging way to get readers to understand what competitive intelligence is and how it adds value to any organization. So, in 2011 they decided to educate business professionals through the power of storytelling. That resulted in their first business book, *New Directions: A Competitive Intelligence Tale*.

"One of the biggest reasons we wrote both books as fictional tales was that we wanted to provide C-suite executives something they would find different and interesting enough to spend their time reading and do so fairly quickly," said Maag.

> ## Marketing With A Bookism
> NEVER TRUST AN AGENCY OWNER WHO HASN'T WRITTEN A BOOK. PERSUADING WITH STORIES IS THE REAL JOB OF AGENCY LEADERSHIP.

©Glasbergen / glasbergen.com

"If I had a bigger office, I'd have room for bigger ideas."

PART III

The What's Next

20

Beware: Rough Seas Ahead

A thought leader I admire, agency owner Drew McLellan, likes to say we as agency owners are captains of our ship.

My warning to my fellow captains: rough waters are ahead. Batten down the hatches as you research, write, publish, and promote your book. If you have something provocative to say, not everyone will agree with you.

(This is my version of Jimmy Fallon's Mean Tweets. One internet troll commented on Amazon about my best-selling book: "Looks like Forbes.com will give a column to any Tom, Dick, or Henry." I am fairly sure he was calling me a dick.)

Call 2022 the collision of brands and politics, a time of vulnerability for every business and author.

> BATTEN DOWN THE HATCHES AS YOU RESEARCH, WRITE, PUBLISH, AND PROMOTE YOUR BOOK. IF YOU HAVE SOMETHING PROVOCATIVE TO SAY, NOT EVERYONE WILL AGREE WITH YOU

"It is time to rethink the relationship between brands and society," says brand expert Jane Cavalier Lucas, author of *The Enchanted Brand: How to Strengthen the Human Side of Business in the Age of New Essentialism* (2022, Indie Books International).

"Traditional brands have sold by selling an aspirational fantasy or identity without accountability, which is now being challenged by the cancel culture," says Lucas.

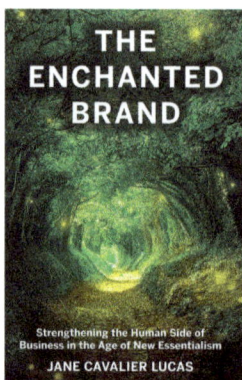

Cover design by William Ramsey

Prior to founding her own agency, BrightMark Consulting, Lucas led strategic planning for clients of McCann Erickson Worldwide, at the time the world's largest advertising agency. At McCann Erickson, she led the rebranding of global companies, including Marriott, Motorola, and US Airways.

Lucas points out we live in a VUCA world—volatile, uncertain, complex, and ambiguous—which is daunting, often terrifying. Because brands are creative conceptual products with the ability to penetrate consciousness, they can strengthen and advance people during this time of vulnerability.

"Brands must serve rather than sell," says Lucas. "To win in a world of complexity, uncertainty, and ambiguity, brands must serve rather than sell and become empowerment tools."

Lucas says the VUCA cancel culture challenge is a variant of the term call-out culture and constitutes a form of boycott typically involving a celebrity who is deemed to have acted or spoken in a questionable or controversial manner.

"Think what has happened to famous authors, talk show hosts, and entertainers in the last two years," says Lucas. "That can happen to brands too."

Lucas, who has taught as an adjunct professor at the Yale School of Management and NYU Stern School of Business, says cancel culture is a modern form of public shaming and ostracism in social media or the real world. It is withdrawing support.

"During the Black Lives Matter protests many brands in the fashion industry were called out for a lack of diversity," says Lucas. "During the pandemic brands like Aunt Jemima, Uncle Ben's, the Washington Redskins, and the Cleveland Indians finally relented to call-out culture."

The days of aspirational fantasy or identity without accountability are over, she says.

"In boom times where the acquisition of things shaped the narrative of success, that brand strategy worked," says Lucas. "However, today we live in a time of contraction, contradiction, and complexity where brands are losing relevancy and value. We need brands to sell differently, to sell by serving the real, hidden needs of people struggling to adapt to a new world."

Lucas says the legacy of commercial brands is vast and includes body shaming (eating disorders didn't just materialize), sexualizing alcohol and cigarettes to promote (over) indulgence, and attaching social elitism to luxury goods (preppy clothes are just the tip of the iceberg). Tied to driving rabid consumerism, brands are partially responsible for driving up personal debt.

"Some brands, however, delivered positive cultural impact and changed lives for the better. Apple inspired personal creativity and growth," says Lucas. "Nike inspired personal drive and growth. We need more of these kinds of brands and now."

Brands can drive responsible consumption by meeting new human needs rather than preying on people's insecurities.

"These are the brands that will achieve the elusive cultural relevance not by spending more, but by serving people more and becoming part of rebuilding society with humanity at the center," says Lucas. "In this new paradigm brands are part of the solution by simply putting the weight of hundreds of billions of dollars of annual cultural messaging into empowering people rather than exploiting them."

Her book has received praise from academics and professionals alike.

"This book is a mind-expanding look at the role brands can play in our new world," says best-selling author Jonah Berger, a marketing professor at the Wharton School at the University of Pennsylvania.

Marketing With A Bookism

EVERYONE HAS THE RIGHT TO THEIR OWN FAITH. WHILE I AM RELIGIOUS, IN CALIFORNIA I TEACH, "THE UNIVERSE REWARDS ACTIVITY." IN THE MIDWEST I TEACH, "THE LORD HELPS THOSE WHO HELP THEMSELVES." I AM BILINGUAL. MY POINT IS, AN AGENCY OWNER WITH A BOOK MUST ADOPT THE MOTTO: "IF IT IS GOING TO BE, IT IS UP TO ME."

21

Thanks A Million

Attracting and retaining great employees is top of mind for every agency owner I interview.

As we come out of the pandemic all companies want to grow. But how can you grow without great people? If you can help companies attract and retain great employees, then you have an offering that can attract high-paying clients.

Inflation, labor and supply upheavals, and a work culture transformation are top of mind for C-suite execs and business owners in 2022, according to The Conference Board's 23rd annual survey of business leaders around the world.[12]

If you charge business leaders more than $10,000 for your services, then you are trying to attract high-paying clients. The best way to land high-paying clients is to help business leaders get what they want.

When it comes to the wants in 2022, labor shortages are driving talent retention and recruitment to the top of the business leader agenda. How do business leaders plan to seize the opportunities?

> THE BEST WAY TO LAND HIGH-PAYING CLIENTS IS TO HELP BUSINESS LEADERS GET WHAT THEY WANT

The Conference Board's *C-Suite Outlook 2022* details the external stress business leaders face and the impact on growth strategies. (The report also explores C-suite views on the benefits and risks of hybrid work models.) The report is based on the views of 1,614 C-suite executives, including 917 international CEOs.

One agency owner who helps business leaders attract top talent is digital marketing agency owner Thomas Young of Intuitive Websites. We met years back when I helped him edit a book on *Winning the Website Wars*. He credits leveraging the book to creating an extra million dollars in revenue per year.

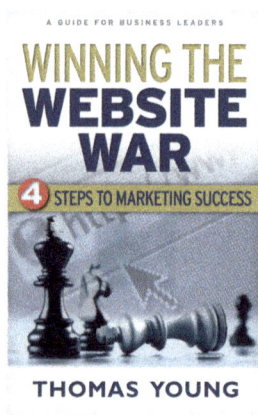

Cover design by Joni McPherson

He has strong advice for how your website can attract great employees.

"Your best job candidates will anonymously visit the home-page of your website, as it is often the starting point of their re-search into your company," says Young. "The homepage must attract not only customers but also these top candidates."

Young is a Vistage CEO peer groups speaker and a

national speaker on digital marketing and website usability. He has presented to thousands about internet marketing in seminars, webinars, and through his podcasts.

Young says the good news is the content on your homepage that attracts quality prospects should also attract your best job candidates. Here are a few key things he advises to capture the attention of qualified job candidates:

Tell a story. First off, have a careers page. "On the careers page, tell a story about working at your company, focus on the benefits and use photos of real people at work," says Young. "Your best job applicants will envision what it is like to work for your company when they visit the website careers page."

No place like home. Homepage content must be relevant to the job candidates too. "Speak the language of the website end-user and focus on what is important to them," says Young. "Keep it simple and avoid large blocks of text. Focus on brief blocks of content with descriptive headers, icons, images, and graphics."

Seek employee help. Get your employees involved. Young advises: "Ask your employees to list the top three reasons why they work for your company and use what you find as key messaging on the careers page."

Talk benefits. No need to be mum about benefits. "Be very clear about the key benefits your company provides," says Young. "This means a lot to job applicants and prospective customers. Do this before you talk about your company's services and products."

Get real. Photos and videos mean a great deal in 2022. "Use photos of real people at your company," says Young.

Avoid obvious clip art photos viewers may see on other companies' websites. He says if you must use clip art photos, make sure to use superior quality photos as they are part of your brand. Use captions on photos to describe your company and include names with people's faces. Get written permission from employees to do this.

Links in the chain. "If possible, link to team member bios and their LinkedIn account," says Young. That's because prospective job candidates like to see who they might be working with. Think of it as social media proof of the company you keep.

Bottom line: "We are in uncharted waters when it comes to recruiting and staffing following the pandemic," says Young. "Companies are looking for help, and their website and digital marketing efforts need to be tools to attract qualified candidates."

Marketing With A Bookism

HUMAN BRAINS ARE HARDWIRED FOR STORIES. WE WANT AND NEED TO HEAR STORIES.

22

Into The Future

Agency owner Justin Breen preaches the gospel, not of agency survival, but of exponential growth.

"I started my company with zero business experience, didn't know what an LLC was, still don't know what S-Corp means, didn't know you had to pay taxes four times a year, and never had heard the word entrepreneur," says Breen. "Now I'm CEO of a global company that only works with the top-mindset businesses and brands in the world."

Breen is CEO of the PR firm BrEpic Communications and author of the best-selling book *Epic Business*. He is an extremely active member of Entrepreneurs' Organization, Strategic Coach, Secret Knock, and ProVisors, and he has an incredible global network of visionaries and exceptional businesses.

Here are some of the top business development growth secrets he has learned since founding his company in 2017:

Network equals net worth. "Having the right mindset attracts the right network. I only partner with people who have visionary, investment, abundance mindsets. Those are the folks who are running the top companies in the world or the ones who will be one day. My company is a giant incubator of geniuses with the right mindset, and they are constantly introducing me to others with investment, visionary, abundance mindsets."

Be a joiner. "Join ultra-high-level groups like Strategic Coach, Abundance360, and Entrepreneurs' Organization; the three groups mentioned are among the top in the world. They include tens of thousands of visionaries—all of them look at things as investments, not costs, and all of them live in abundance, not scarcity. The groups weed out all the wrong-fit people and clients. When you are in groups, everything is collaborative, and entrepreneurs rise together."

The bottom line for Breen is to embrace the future. "I'm a futurist, meaning things I said years ago are happening now."

How Not To Run Afoul Of Fair Use

Writing books is a great agency marketing technique. But what is fair when it comes to quoting the copyrighted works of others?

Before we part, I must share a word of warning about marketing with a book for agencies.

There is a saying used by the faculty members at my university: "Stealing from one person is called plagiarism, and you will get fired. Stealing from many, and citing sources, is called research, and you will get tenure."

The legal concept of "fair use" in the digital age is in the news. The issue is how much one person or company can use the intellectual property of another without having to pay royalties.

Some seasoned journalists talk about using a 250-word rule of thumb when quoting from a book. But is that kosher?

"Copyright law does not include a 250-word fair use safe harbor," says Joy Butler, attorney and author of *The Permission Seeker's Guide through the Legal Jungle.* "The origin of this copyright law myth is that publishers sometimes choose to give blanket permission allowing others to cite up to 250 words of a work. Authors should not assume that the publisher of the work to be quoted employs the 250-word practice."

Butler says fair use is a qualitative and not a quantitative test. An author who wants to rely on fair use can heed this rule of thumb:

Use the quotation for purposes of commentary, news reporting, or parody—though that need not be the primary purpose of your entire article or book. Quote as few words as possible to make your point. Note your fair use chances increase when quoting a factual work like history rather than highly creative work like a science fiction novel.

QUOTE AS FEW WORDS AS POSSIBLE TO MAKE YOUR POINT

Oh, and don't quote song lyrics. There is no fair use without permission for that great Willie Nelson or Lady Gaga lyric. When in doubt, get permission. When not in doubt, get permission.

New Clients Do Judge A Book By Its Cover

Yes, the old cliché is true: people judge a book by its cover. They also judge the author by the entire book design. That is especially true when you choose to independently publish your book.

Independent publishing is an alternative to traditional

publishing that helps business thought leaders create impact and influence. If you want to independently publish a book to attract new clients for your agency, consulting practice, or other trusted advisor-type business, you need to make the book look as professional as possible.

The world does not need another crummy-looking self-published book.

The right print book can be the number one marketing tool for agency principals, strategic consultants, and business coaches. According to an April 2022 Statista article using data from *Publishers Weekly*, US print book sales have been on the rise since 2012.[13] A 2021 Pew Research study found that 32 percent of Americans only read print books, as opposed to just 9 percent who only consume digital books and 33 percent who consume both.[14] Furthermore, Statista found that in 2021, only 23.4 percent of the US population bought an e-book, while 44.6 percent bought a print book.

Rachel Valliere is a book designer, consultant, and founder of Printed Page Studios. Over the last twelve years, she has worked on hundreds of book projects with a variety of publishing companies and individual authors. She specializes in nonfiction book covers and interior design. Here are her top five tips for attracting new clients with a well-designed book:

Use a professional designer. "If your book is anything more than a hobby, professional book design is nonnegotiable," says Valliere. "Think of it this way—if you landed an interview for your dream job, would you show up in sweatpants? There's nothing inherently wrong with sweatpants—they wouldn't stop you from being the best candidate on earth for the job—but you'll be judged on that first impression. Fair or not, your book will be judged the same way."

Listen to your designer. "They're getting paid for a reason," says Valliere. "It's true that design is subjective, but it's also true that design skills are built on a foundation of relatively objective principles that take time and experience to develop. It's important that your designer collaborates with you to create a cover you love, but you'll end up with the best result if you trust their opinion and try to relinquish control of the details."

Treat your book cover as a marketing tool. "Although it's very personal, your book cover is product packaging," says Valliere. "When making decisions about the design, it's crucial to look through the lens of your target audience and think about what would connect with them. Make sure that all design decisions are intentional and focused primarily on what your audience will resonate with, rather than your personal style preferences."

Capitalize on book interior features to boost engagement. "Include a marketing page with a clear call to action and your contact information," says Valliere. "Use QR codes to drive traffic to your website, booking page, or supplemental downloadable resources. Include pull quotes to help break up the text and highlight key takeaways, so readers can flip through and get an idea of the content."

Publish a print version, not just an e-book. "Aside from adding legitimacy, a print version is wonderful to showcase and

INCLUDE PULL QUOTES TO HELP BREAK UP THE TEXT AND HIGHLIGHT KEY TAKEAWAYS, SO READERS CAN FLIP THROUGH AND GET AN IDEA OF THE CONTENT

pass out for marketing purposes," says Valliere. "It's also better for sales."

Bottom line: The print book is alive and doing well. If you are willing to write the right book to increase your impact and influence, make sure you publish a book that makes a great impression.

And In Closing

This might be my last book. But this is not the last word I have to say on the subject.

Please check out what I have to say weekly on Forbes. com. Please join one of my no-cost roundtable discussions I host on Zoom eight times a year. Attend one of my three-hour master classes on writing the right book that I conduct on Zoom five times a year. If you have a book you want to leverage, apply to attend one of my three public two-day virtual author retreats. You can learn about these on my website, Indie-BooksIntl.com/events.

If you have an idea for a Forbes.com column, I would love to hear it. Please understand, I can't say yes to everyone. You can start the conversation by sending an email to henry@indiebooksintl.com with the subject line Forbes.com.

IF YOU HAVE AN IDEA FOR A FORBES.COM COLUMN, I WOULD LOVE TO HEAR IT

If you are ever open to a conversation about advice on publishing a book to market your agency, that would be most welcome.

Marketing With A Bookism

HOWEVER OUR PATHS CROSS, I LOOK FORWARD TO BEING HELPFUL TO YOU IN SOME WAY. WHEN IT COMES TO BOOKS AND AGENCY OWNERS, MY BRAND IS GENEROSITY.

APPENDIX

APPENDIX A
MARKETING WITH A BOOK MODEL

Publishing a book is the starting line for agency business development, not the finish line. And what is the best way to get to the starting line with a book that can create a 400 percent to 2,000 percent ROI? Here are the steps to follow:

1. Select Target Rich Niche. The narrower the focus, the more powerful the appeal. Be interesting to fewer prospects and have them be more intensely interested in your agency.

2. Conduct Proprietary Research. Gather secondary data from others, undertake an extensive literature review of books and journal articles, and conduct primary interviews where possible. Buy a dozen books on your subject and capture two dozen articles. Conduct in-depth interviews with prospects on the subject.

3. Determine Your Number One Problem. Be a heat-seeking missile for the number one pain of your prospects. Record interviews and focus group sessions to use their exact words.

4. Create Proprietary Problem-Solving Process. Typically, six to eight steps, principles, or practices. Name it the blank-blank method, system, process, or methodology. Write down your tips, tactics, advice, and strategy. Then start sorting by putting them into six to eight buckets of related information.

5. Choose Which Of The Eight Great Stories For Overarching Story. These are monster, underdog, comedy, tragedy, mystery, quest, rebirth, or escape. Typically, agency books are about monster problems, mysteries, quests, or rebirths.

6. Create Outline With Working Title, Subtitle, And Contents. This is the writing road map, but I prefer to call it a blueprint. Books are built like houses are built. Do not try to write by seat-of-the-pants inspiration.

7. Draft The Sloppy First Copy. Any book worth writing is worth writing a first draft that sucks. The magic will be in the rewrite. But first, you must get it out of your head and onto paper. Consider recording from the outline and transcribing because this is ten times faster and has more energy.

CONSIDER RECORDING FROM OUTLINE AND TRANSCRIBING BECAUSE THIS IS TEN TIMES FASTER AND HAS MORE ENERGY

8. Write Part I, The Why. Typically, two chapters: why the problem matters and how to solve it in general (an overview of your proprietary process).

9. Write Part II, The How. Typically, six to eight chapters examining the parts of the proprietary process in detail. Name the process. Put on the copyright page that you intend to trademark. Prospects respect process.

10. Write Part III, What's Next. Typically, two chapters about sustaining the process, or creating a culture, and a forecast for the future.

11. Solicit Qualified Feedback For Second Draft. This is the role of a developmental editor. Choose someone who is qualified. If you want beta readers too, that is fine; it just adds time to the process.

12. Rewrite Magical Second Draft. The magic is in the rewrite.

13. Submit Publishable Manuscript For Publication. This is the version the author and the developmental editor are happy with. But this is not the last chance you have for revision.

14. Gather Feedback From Professional Copyeditors. Get more qualified eyes on the book, especially a qualified *Chicago Manual of Style* editor.

15. Create Book Front Cover Design. In conjunction with step 14, work with an art director on cover design. This needs to be completed before you can proceed to step 16.

16. Submit Approved Manuscript To Art Director. Now you have crossed out of the realm of Microsoft Word document edits to a designed layout.

17. Solicit Foreword And Testimonials. Use the Microsoft Word document from step 16 to solicit someone to write a foreword and other notables to endorse the book with a back cover blurb. This happens simultaneously as art director is laying out galleys.

18. Review Twenty-Page Design Mockup. Provide detailed feedback to the art director for the look of the book (I use an eighteen-point checklist; see appendix).

19. Art Director Creates Full Galley. With the feedback from step 18 the art director can create the whole book.

20. Proof Full Galley. Author's team and the publisher's team must proof the manuscript in detail for gremlins. Rewriting at this stage costs extra money.

21. Produce Print-On-Demand Paperback Book. Submit approved PDFs to publishing service.

22. Produce e-Book. Submit approved PDFs to e-Book publishing service.

23. Produce Hardback Book. Submit flyleaf cover design and book PDFs to hardback book publishing service.

24. Produce Audiobook. Audition readers and have audio editors produce digital files.

25. Conduct Soft Launch Campaign. There is a time between when the book is available for purchase as a paperback on Amazon.com and all formats of the book are available. This is known as the soft launch period and can take up to sixty days.

26. Conduct Hard Launch Campaign. Consider running a ninety-nine-cent Kindle e-book campaign of one to two weeks to gather verified purchase reviews on Amazon. Buyers judge books by the number of reviews. First goal is two dozen reviews, second goal is more than one hundred reviews. Also consider hosting a live or virtual launch event to generate buzz. If you do not treat the book launch like it is a big deal, how will others think it is a big deal?

27. Schedule And Deliver Small-Scale Seminars. These can be live or on Zoom. Consider hosting six to twelve a year. Objective is five to ten people in discussion about the book topic. Use LinkedIn to find your target audience.

28. Solicit Publicity And Podcast Appearances. Write and distribute a national news release. Solicit a minimum of two podcast interviews a month about the book.

29. Begin Monthly Sample Book Mailings. Do not wait for the book to be discovered. Mail a minimum of twenty gift copies of the book each month to people who can book you as a speaker, book you as a podcast guest, hire your agency, or write about the information in the book.

30. Lather, Rinse, Repeat. Consistency trumps blitzkrieg campaigns. Think tortoise and hare fable: slow and steady wins the race. Agency business development is a marathon, not a 100-meter dash.

APPENDIX B
BOOK BLUEPRINT PROCESS

The Indie Books International Book BluePrint Process is a twelve-week intensive developmental editing program. It is not only possible to write a great nonfiction business book or brief business novella in twelve weeks; it is preferable to produce a first draft within this time. A fast first draft capitalizes on momentum, minimizes the urge to self-edit and get caught in the perfectionism trap too early in the writing process, and ensures that our authors get on track, stay on pace, and remain on a path to publication.

Step 1: Scope, Title, Subtitle

1. Scope the project. Discuss the author/speaker/consultant's expertise, subject domain, proprietary system, angle, customers, and pains they solve. Find the working title. If scope is too large for one book, excise the main idea for the first book; set other ideas in the parking lot for potential *future blueprints*.

2. One blueprint/book/idea at a time, sequentially. (We do not, of course, control what an author does in his/her free time; however, Indie Books does not recommend simultaneous book-writing and we do not schedule simultaneous book development services with the same author.)

3. Working title. Should be a trifecta and work as a speech title, book subtitle, and URL (check domain registration availability).

a. What is the name of your business? Is it clear what you do? Is your name a part of the business?

b. In eleven words or less, who is your target client and what result do you achieve for them?

c. What are the pains, worries, and frustrations that you help clients deal with?

d. What is your solution for helping clients? Do you have a model, methodology, or proprietary process?

e. What is the common misperception that holds many potential clients back from overcoming their pains, worries, and frustrations?

f. What do your prospective clients need to do in general to solve their problems that you are the expert in? In other words, do you have basic steps that most clients should follow?

g. In addition to solving their main problem, what other benefits do clients receive from following the course of action that you advocate?

h. Now, and only now, that you have answered the preceding questions are you ready to brainstorm a working title for your book.

   Examples:

   i. *7 Dumb Things We All Say*

   ii. *Better Implementation Now!*

   iii. *Bad Behavior, People Problems, and Sticky Situations*

   iv. *CEO Point Blank*

     v.   *Contentious Custody*

     vi. *Why Can't I Hire Good People?*

     vii. *The Agile-Minded Executive*

     viii. *Taming the Compensation Monster*

4. Working subtitle: Answers "What's in it for me?" (WIIFM) for target audience. *Who is the book for and what is the outcome they want?*

Examples:

a. *The Science of Attracting High-Paying Clients for Consultants and Coaches*

b. *How Smart Dentists Crack the Code and Build a Dream Practice*

c. *A Toolbook for Managers and Team Leaders*

d. *Building Cross-Cultural Relationships that Last*

e. *Market Yourself Effectively and Accelerate Your Results*

f. *Profiting from the Coming Surge in Women's Sexual Health and Wellness*

g. *The Formula for Becoming and Staying a Top-Producing Franchisee*

h. *The Experts' Guide to Placing Articles in Print and Online*

Step 2: The Table of Contents (TOC) Outline

The Table of Contents is the highest-level outline of the book manuscript. It need not be fully developed to begin a draft, but it ideally should be complete before deep writing begins, as it helps to clarify your vision and direction.

Nonfiction Business Book: Three Parts, Ten Chapters, Eight Stories, Infinite Possibilities

The nonfiction business book is the most common type, and even so, it is a *story*. The BluePrint process will help the author identify which type of story they are telling and map it to a structure that readers and prospects will find compelling.

There Are Eight Stories In The World. What's Yours?

Monster. A terrifying, all-powerful, life-threatening monster whom the hero or heroine must confront in a fight to the death.

Underdog. Someone who has seemed to the world quite commonplace is shown to have been hiding a second, more exceptional self within.

Quest. From the moment the hero or heroine learns of the priceless goal, he or she sets out on a hazardous journey to reach it.

Escape. The hero or heroine and a few companions travel out of the familiar surroundings into another world completely cut off from the first. While it is at first wonderful, there is a sense of increasing peril. After a dramatic escape, they return to the familiar world where they began.

Comedy. A chaos of misunderstanding, the characters tie themselves and each other into a knot that seems almost unbearable; however, to universal relief, everyone and everything gets sorted out, bringing about a happy ending.

Tragedy. This is about solving a problem by going against the laws of nature, society, or God. A character through some flaw or lack of self-understanding is increasingly drawn into a fatal course of action that leads inexorably to disaster. These are cautionary tales.

Rebirth. There is a mounting sense of threat as a dark force approaches the hero until it emerges completely, holding the hero in its deadly grip. Only after a time, when the dark force has triumphed, does the reversal take place.

Mystery. This appeared in the time of Edgar Allan Poe. From Sherlock Holmes to *CSI: Miami*, the plot that involves solving a riddle has gained immense popularity in the last 150 years.

Nonfiction Book Part 1 (3,000–5,000 words): The Why?

Chapter 1: Why [Topic] Matters:

In 1,500–2,500 words, lay out a (brief!) compelling argument to give prospects/readers a reason to read further. Establish the WIIFM here, and make it *hurt*—but also make it interesting, intriguing. Bring up angles they may never have thought of before, surprising facts, novel developments—anything your unique expertise can offer to illuminate the topic.

Chapter 2: Solution In General + Author's Mess-To-Success Story

Use 1,500–2,500 words. Now that they're hurting, take the pain away, but *in general*. Not too specific. Not too soon. Let them know there's hope. You've found it. But first, you had to go through trials and tribulations.

And here is where you describe them specifically, as they relate to discovering the secret to stopping that pain. It's not necessarily a full autobiography; it's a relevant professional autobiography—a reason for readers to trust you to solve their problems because after they've read this chapter, they've seen you do it. They just may not have seen quite *how* yet.

Nonfiction Book Part 2 (12,000 to 24,000 words total): The How?

This is the area with the greatest variability and less is more. We do not recommend overwhelming readers with the depth and breadth of your expertise. Brief 1,500-to-2,500-word chapters are ideal for a quick read. If you feel compelled to write more, *great, but that is not necessary.*

Chapters 3 Through 8 (1,500 to 2,500 words per chapter)

Six chapters. Six buckets of content. Six stages of your proprietary system, process, or solution. (Although this is the shortest entry in this document, it will be the longest, most labor-intensive part of the BluePrint work process, because it is intensive and unique to each client.)

Nonfiction Book Part 3 (3,000–5,000 words total): The What's Next?

Chapter 9: Sustaining Or Maintaining Gains

In stories, a hero brings treasures and gifts to the people. In this case, the boons you bring to your clients will need to be maintained and sustained. Chapter 9 tells them what they will need to do once their coach/consultant/hero (you) are no longer with them. It is the chapter that promises, "This is not a flash in the pan. This is a self-contained system, capable of surviving beyond and without me."

Chapter 10: Troubleshooting And Summary

The concluding chapter is the end of the line. The farewell. The "What to do when things go wrong" and the bidding of luck and good fortune. The wrap-up and a *reminder that you are always there for them*. (Pssst. That's the troubleshooting.)

Option: Nonfiction Business Parable/Fable/ Novella

The nonfiction business fable tells a story about a character to teach a greater truth. Its roots go back as far as humans sitting around campfires regaling each other with tales of the hunt (to share wisdom about how not to get trampled by a mastodon the next time, like poor, clumsy Oog, may he rest in peace). Its most famous analog is, of course, the biblical parable. In business books, we ask who moved whose cheese, who's sitting in what seats on which bus, and many other questions based on extended fables, metaphors, and analogies.

The fable can stand as a unique, memorable platform for speeches and a proprietary consulting platform in nonquantitative disciplines.

APPENDIX C
ACKNOWLEDGMENTS

I wish to express gratitude to the agency owners and marketing consultants who are advocates of my work. These include Brandon Prather, Bryan Gray, Clare Price, Craig Lowder, Dan Janal, Darren LaCroix, David Newman, Drew McLellan, Ed Tate, Eleni Kelakos, Ellen Melko Moore, Justin Breen, Lisa Apolinski, Marisa Vallbona, Mark Brown, Mark LeBlanc, Michelle Stansbury, Nona Prather, Patrick McGowan, Penny Reed, Russell Trahan, Scott Hamilton, Stephen Woessner, Theresa Ashby, Tom Searcy, and Thomas Young,

In addition, gratitude goes to my many mentors who have recently passed: professor Glen Broom of San Diego State University, the world's leading public relations scholar, for four decades of mentoring and friendship; *Chino Champion* newspaper publisher Al McCombs, who gave me, at the age of fifteen, my first paying job as a writer; first coauthor Diane Gage Lofgren, who in 1990 taught me to be a coauthor; and professor Jack Douglass of UC San Diego, who in 1975 gladly took this teenager straight off a farm under his wing and taught me how to create the career of my dreams. I miss you all truly, deeply.

I want to thank the forgotten agency owner who taught me my favorite agency owner joke.[15]

Also I want to thank the team at Indie Books International, including Adrienne Moch, Alan Dino Hebel, Ann LeBlanc, Bill Ramsey, Denise Montgomery, Devin DeVries, Don Sevrens, Eric Guidas, Gail Sevrens, Heather Pendley, Ian Koviak, Jack DeVries, Joni McPherson, Jordan DeVries, Laura Duffy, Lisa Lucas, Mark LeBlanc, Rachel Valliere, Sally

Romoser, Steve Plummer, Suzanne Hagen, Taylor Graham, and Vikki DeVries and so many others who have helped me create my masterpiece: a business that is the Apple Computer of agency owner books, making it easy and affordable for every agency to have more credibility, more impact, and more influence.

To my Heavenly Father, thank you for helping me expand my territory so I can serve more of your other agency owner children to get what they want in life.[16] Thank you to the hundreds of authors, vendors, and investors who chose Indie Books International.

APPENDIX D
ABOUT THE AUTHOR

Henry DeVries, MBA, is the weekly business development columnist with Forbes.com and the CEO of Indie Books International, an Oceanside, California company he cofounded in 2014 to work with small to midsized agency owners and marketing consultants who want to attract high-paying clients by marketing with a book and speech (www.indiebooksintl.com). In his writing and speaking he shares in humorous ways many pragmatic strategies that can double sales and achieve marketing returns of 400 percent to 2,000 percent. Previously he served as assistant dean of continuing education for UC San Diego. Prior to that he helped double revenues as president of an award-winning *Ad Age 500* advertising agency and was a vice president that doubled awareness for a $5 billion insurance company. Since 2010, he has ghostwritten, coauthored, and published more than 300 business books, including his McGraw-Hill bestseller *How to Close a Deal like Warren Buffett*—now in five languages, including Chinese. In 1999 he founded the New Client Marketing Institute to study how agencies and consultants attract right-fit clients. This is the seventeenth book he has published to share his research findings. He earned his bachelor's degree from UC San Diego and his MBA from San Diego State University and has completed two certificate programs at the Harvard Business School. On a personal note, Henry is a baseball nut. A former Associated Press sportswriter, he has visited forty-four major league ballparks and has three to go before he "touches 'em all."

He can be reached at henry@indiebooksintl.com. Learn more about Henry at his LinkedIn page: https://www.linkedin.com/in/henryjdevries or by visiting the website for Indie Books International: http://indiebooksintl.com.

Other Books By Henry DeVries:

Self-Marketing Secrets (with Diane Gage)

Pain Killer Marketing (with Chris Stiehl)

Client Seduction (with Denise Bryson)

Closing America's Job Gap (with Mary Walshok and Tapan Monroe)

Marketing the Marketers

How to Close a Deal Like Warren Buffett (with Tom Searcy)

Marketing with a Book

Persuade with a Story!

Client Attraction Chain Reaction

Build Your Consulting Practice (with Mark LeBlanc)

Defining You (with Mark LeBlanc and Kathy McAfee)

Persuade with a Case Acceptance Story! (with Penny Reed and Mark LeBlanc)

Persuade with a Digital Content Story! (with Lisa Apolinski)

Rainmaker Confidential (with Scott Love and Mark LeBlanc)

Bringing In the Business (to be published in 2023, with David Goldman and Mark LeBlanc)

Trusted Advisor Confidential (to be published in 2023, with Craig Lowder)

WORKS CITED

AND AUTHOR'S NOTES

1   "Marketing Agency Growth Report 2018" by HubSpot was a survey of 763 agencies in the United States, Canada, and United Kingdom, with 70 percent of respondents at the director level and 51 percent at the owner/president level. The report, and other surveys, are offered for free at offers.hubspot.com.

2   The work of the now-retired David Maister, PhD, was a game changer for me. I recommend his website davidmaister.com. Also, his books such as *Managing the Professional Service Firm* (New York: Free Press, 1997) and *The Trusted Advisor: 20th Anniversary Edition* (New York: Free Press, 2021) are important works to study. With his blessing, I took one page from one of his books and built my twenty-year proprietary research study around it. Many of my books are dedicated to Maister.

3   This is the seventeenth book I have written on the research findings of the New Client Marketing Institute, which I founded in 1999 while serving on the continuing education faculty of UC San Diego, where I eventually became assistant dean of continuing education. Some of my books to read for research details include *Client Seduction* (with Denise Bryson, Bloomington, IN: AuthorHouse, 2005), *Client Attraction Chain Reaction* (San Diego: Indie Books International, 2020), and *Rainmaker Confidential* (with Scott Love and Mark LeBlanc, San Diego: Indie Books International, 2021).

4   For help learning how to do this, please see my website, PersuadeWithAStory.com.

5   Ben Dattner, "Cobblers Children Syndrome in the Workplace," website of *Psychology Today*, posted December 6, 2008, https://www.psychologytoday.com/us/blog/credit-and-blame-work/200812/cobblers-children-syndrome-in-the-workplace.

6   Drew McLellan and Stephen Woessner, *Sell With Authority* (Des Moines, IA: BookPress Publishing, 2020).

7   For example, there are 7,900 US agencies with five to two hundred employees in our database. David C. Baker has been a mentor of mine for twenty years. I recommend all his five books, especially *The Business of Expertise* (Nashville: RockBench Publishing Corp., 2017).

8   Christopher Booker of the United Kingdom was a founding editor of *Private Eye*, to which he regularly contributed, and also wrote a longstanding column for

the *Sunday Telegraph*. His best-selling books include *The Seven Basic Plots: Why We Tell Stories* (London: Bloomsbury, 2005), *The Real Global Warming Disaster* (London: Bloomsbury, 2013), *The Great Deception* (with Richard North, London: Bloomsbury, 2016), and *The Mad Officials* (with Richard North, London: Constable, 1994). Booker died in July 2019. The publisher said *The Seven Basic Plots* answers "whether there are only a small number of 'basic stories' in the world. Using a wealth of examples, from ancient myths and folk tales via the plays and novels of great literature to the popular movies and TV soap operas of today, it shows that there are seven archetypal themes [Booker said an eighth was added 150 years ago with the mystery], which recur throughout every kind of storytelling. But this is only the prelude to an investigation into how and why we are 'programmed' to imagine stories in these ways, and how they relate to the inmost patterns of human psychology." I say Hollywood only makes eight movies because human brains are hardwired to want and need to hear these eight stories.

9   Baker, *Business of Expertise*.

10   Jeremy Hsu, "The Secrets of Storytelling: Why We Love a Good Yarn," website of Scientific American, August 1, 2008, https://www.scientificamerican.com/article/the-secrets-of-storytelling/.

11   Chris Stiehl and Henry DeVries, *Pain Killer Marketing* (El Monte, CA: WBusiness Books, 2008).

12   https://www.conference-board.org/topics/c-suite-outlook.

13   Amy Watson, "U.S. book industry – statistics & facts," Statista.com, April 11, 2022, https://www.statista.com/topics/1177/book-market/.

14   Michelle Faverio and Andrew Perrin, "Three-in-ten Americans now read e-books," Pew Research Center, January 6, 2022.

15   My favorite agency owner joke: One Monday afternoon after a rough day at work, an ad agency owner, his art director, and his copywriter walk into a bar to grab a well-deserved drink together.

Not wanting to be bothered, they take the booth in the back corner, but as they get comfortable, the trio find an antique-looking oil lamp. Jokingly, the agency owner picks it up and rubs it, but much to their surprise a genie really appears.

With wide eyes they merely watch the genie stretch out before he looks at them and says, "Just because you let me stretch my limbs a bit, I will grant each of you one wish."

The art director gets excited and almost falls from her chair as she asks the genie to pick her first. "Please, I want to be a rich and famous artist with a studio on the Left Bank in Paris."

Poof! In a puff of smoke, the art director vanishes, and the copywriter eagerly asks for a chance to go next. "I have always wanted to write the Great American novel, live in Cape Cod, and wear a sports coat with elbow patches."

And just like that, poof! The copywriter disappears in a puff of smoke as well. Since that leaves only the agency owner, the genie turns to him and says, "All right, it's your turn to state your wish."

The agency owner says, "We have to pitch the Bixby account this week. I want those two jerks back at work right now."

Poof!

16 Thank you Rabbi Daniel Lapin, for that first secret from your book *Business Secrets from the Bible* (Hoboken, NJ: Wiley, 2014): "God wants each of us to be obsessively preoccupied with the needs and desires of his other children." I am preoccupied with his agency owner children.

INDEX